JAMESTOWN EDUCATION

Timed Readings Plus *in Science*

25 Two-Part Lessons
with Questions for
Building Reading Speed and Comprehension

BOOK 10

Mc Graw Hill **Glencoe McGraw-Hill**

New York, New York   Columbus, Ohio   Chicago, Illinois   Peoria, Illinois   Woodland Hills, California

JAMESTOWN EDUCATION

Glencoe/McGraw-Hill

A Division of The McGraw·Hill Companies

ISBN: 0-07-827379-X

Send all queries to:
Glencoe/McGraw-Hill
8787 Orion Place
Columbus, OH 43240-4027

1 2 3 4 5 6 7 8 9 10   021   08 07 06 05 04 03 02

CONTENTS

You probably talk at an average rate of about 150 words a minute. If you are a reader of average ability, you read at a rate of about 250 words a minute. So your reading speed is nearly twice as fast as your speaking or listening speed. This example shows that reading is one of the fastest ways to get information.

The purpose of this book is to help you increase your reading rate and understand what you read. The 25 lessons in this book will also give you practice in reading science articles and in preparing for tests in which you must read and understand nonfiction passages within a certain time limit.

Reading Faster and Better

Following are some strategies that you can use to read the articles in each lesson.

Previewing

Previewing before you read is a very important step. This helps you to get an idea of what a selection is about and to recall any previous knowledge you have about the subject. Here are the steps to follow when previewing.

Read the title. Titles are designed not only to announce the subject but also to make the reader think. Ask yourself questions such as What can I learn from the title? What thoughts does it bring to mind?

What do I already know about this subject?

Read the first sentence. If they are short, read the first two sentences. The opening sentence is the writer's opportunity to get your attention. Some writers announce what they hope to tell you in the selection. Some writers state their purpose for writing; others just try to get your attention.

Read the last sentence. If it is short, read the final two sentences. The closing sentence is the writer's last chance to get ideas across to you. Some writers repeat the main idea once more. Some writers draw a conclusion—this is what they have been leading up to. Other writers summarize their thoughts; they tie all the facts together.

Skim the entire selection. Glance through the selection quickly to see what other information you can pick up. Look for anything that will help you read fluently and with understanding. Are there names, dates, or numbers? If so, you may have to read more slowly.

Reading for Meaning

Here are some ways to make sure you are making sense of what you read.

Build your concentration. You cannot understand what you read if you are not concentrating. When you discover that your thoughts are straying, correct the situation right away. Avoid distractions and distracting situations. Keep in mind the information you learned from previewing. This will help focus your attention on the selection.

Read in thought groups. Try to see meaningful combinations of words—phrases, clauses, or sentences. If you look at only one word at a time (called word-by-word reading), both your comprehension and your reading speed suffer.

Ask yourself questions. To sustain the pace you have set for yourself and to maintain a high level of concentration and comprehension, ask yourself questions such as What does this mean? or How can I use this information? as you read.

Finding the Main Ideas

The paragraph is the basic unit of meaning. If you can quickly discover and understand the main idea of each paragraph, you will build your comprehension of the selection.

Find the topic sentence. The topic sentence, which contains the main idea, often is the first sentence of a paragraph. It is followed by sentences that support, develop, or explain the main idea. Sometimes a topic sentence comes at the end of a paragraph. When it does, the supporting details come first, building the base for the topic sentence. Some paragraphs do not have a topic sentence; all of the sentences combine to create a meaningful idea.

Understand paragraph structure. Every well-written paragraph has a purpose. The purpose may be to inform, define, explain or illustrate. The purpose should always relate to the main idea and expand on it. As you read each paragraph, see how the body of the paragraph tells you more about the main idea.

Relate ideas as you read. As you read the selection, notice how the writer puts together ideas. As you discover the relationship between the ideas, the main ideas come through quickly and clearly.

Mastering Reading Comprehension

Reading fast is not useful if you don't remember or understand what you read. The two exercises in Part A provide a check on how well you have understood the article.

Recalling Facts

These multiple-choice questions provide a quick check to see how well you recall important information from the article. As you learn to apply the reading strategies described earlier, you should be able to answer these questions more successfully.

Understanding Ideas

These questions require you to think about the main ideas in the article. Some main ideas are stated in the article; others are not. To answer some of the questions, you need to draw conclusions about what you read.

The five exercises in Part B require multiple answers. These exercises provide practice in applying comprehension and critical-thinking skills that you can use in all your reading.

Recognizing Words in Context

Always check to see whether the words around an unfamiliar word—its context—can give you a clue to the word's meaning. A word generally appears in a context related to its meaning.

Suppose, for example, that you are unsure of the meaning of the word *expired* in the following passage:

> Vera wanted to check out a book, but her library card had expired. She had to borrow my card, because she didn't have time to renew hers.

You could begin to figure out the meaning of *expired* by asking yourself a question such as, What could have happened to Vera's library card that would make her need to borrow someone else's card? You might realize that if Vera had to renew her card, its usefulness must have come to an end or run out. This would lead you to conclude that the word *expired* must mean "to come to an end" or "to run out." You would be right. The context suggested the meaning.

Context can also affect the meaning of a word you already know. The word *key,* for instance, has many meanings. There are musical keys, door keys, and keys to solving a mystery. The context in which the word *key* occurs will tell you which meaning is correct.

Sometimes a word is explained by the words that immediately follow it. The subject of a sentence and your knowledge about that subject might also help you determine the meaning of an unknown word. Try to decide the meaning of the word *revive* in the following sentence:

> Sunshine and water will revive those drooping plants.

The compound subject is *sunshine* and *water*. You know that plants need light and water to survive and that drooping plants are not healthy. You can figure out that *revive* means "to bring back to health."

Distinguishing Fact from Opinion

Every day you are called upon to sort out fact and opinion. Because much of what you read and hear contains both facts and opinions, you need to be able to tell the two apart.

Facts are statements that can be proved true. The proof must be objective and verifiable. You must be able to check for yourself to confirm a fact.

Look at the following facts. Notice that they can be checked for accuracy and confirmed. Suggested sources for verification appear in parentheses.

- Abraham Lincoln was the 16th president of the United States. (Consult biographies, social studies books, encyclopedias, and similar sources.)

- Earth revolves around the Sun.
  (Research in encyclopedias
  or astronomy books; ask
  knowledgeable people.)

- Dogs walk on four legs.
  (See for yourself.)

Opinions are statements that
cannot be proved true. There is no
objective evidence you can consult
to check the truthfulness of an opinion. Unlike facts, opinions express
personal beliefs or judgments. Opinions reveal how someone feels about
a subject, not the facts about that
subject. You might agree or disagree
with someone's opinion, but you
cannot prove it right or wrong.

Look at the following opinions.
The reasons these statements are classified as opinions appear in parentheses.

- Abraham Lincoln was born to be a
  president. (You cannot prove this by
  referring to birth records. There is
  no evidence to support this belief.)

- Earth is the only planet in our
  solar system where intelligent life
  exists. (There is no proof of this. It
  may be proved true some day, but
  for now it is just an educated
  guess—not a fact.)

- The dog is a human's best friend.
  (This is not a fact; your best friend
  might not be a dog.)

As you read, be aware that facts and
opinions are often mixed together.
Both are useful to you as a reader. But
to evaluate what you read and to read
intelligently, you need to know the difference between the two.

Keeping Events in Order

Sequence, or chronological order, is
the order of events in a story or
article or the order of steps in a
process. Paying attention to the
sequence of events or steps will help
you follow what is happening,
predict what might happen next,
and make sense of a passage.

To make the sequence as clear as
possible, writers often use signal
words to help the reader get a more
exact idea of when things happen.
Following is a list of frequently used
signal words and phrases:

until	first
next	then
before	after
finally	later
when	while
during	now
at the end	by the time
as soon as	in the beginning

Signal words and phrases are also
useful when a writer chooses to
relate details or events out of
sequence. You need to pay careful
attention to determine the correct
chronological order.

Making Correct Inferences

Much of what you read *suggests* more
than it *says*. Writers often do not
state ideas directly in a text. They
can't. Think of the time and space it
would take to state every idea. And
think of how boring that would be!
Instead, writers leave it to you, the
reader, to fill in the information they
leave out—to make inferences. You
do this by combining clues in the

story or article with knowledge from your own experience.

You make many inferences every day. Suppose, for example, that you are visiting a friend's house for the first time. You see a bag of kitty litter. You infer (make an inference) that the family has a cat. Another day you overhear a conversation. You catch the names of two actors and the words *scene, dialogue,* and *directing.* You infer that the people are discussing a movie or play.

In these situations and others like them, you infer unstated information from what you observe or read. Readers must make inferences in order to understand text.

Be careful about the inferences you make. One set of facts may suggest several inferences. Some of these inferences could be faulty. A correct inference must be supported by evidence.

Remember that bag of kitty litter that caused you to infer that your friend has a cat? That could be a faulty inference. Perhaps your friend's family uses the kitty litter on their icy sidewalks to create traction. To be sure your inference is correct, you need more evidence.

Understanding Main Ideas

The main idea is the most important idea in a paragraph or passage—the idea that provides purpose and direction. The rest of the selection explains, develops, or supports the main idea. Without a main idea, there would be only a collection of unconnected thoughts.

In the following paragraph, the main idea is printed in italics. As you read, observe how the other sentences develop or explain the main idea.

Typhoon Chris hit with full fury today on the central coast of Japan. Heavy rain from the storm flooded the area. High waves carried many homes into the sea. People now fear that the heavy rains will cause mudslides in the central part of the country. The number of people killed by the storm may climb past the 200 mark by Saturday.

In this paragraph, the main-idea statement appears first. It is followed by sentences that explain, support, or give details. Sometimes the main idea appears at the end of a paragraph. Writers often put the main idea at the end of a paragraph when their purpose is to persuade or convince. Readers may be more open to a new idea if the reasons for it are presented first.

As you read the following paragraph, think about the overall impact of the supporting ideas. Their purpose is to convince the reader that the main idea in the last sentence should be accepted.

Last week there was a head-on collision at Huntington and Canton streets. Just a month ago a pedestrian was struck there. Fortunately, she was only slightly injured. In the past year, there have been more accidents there than at any other corner in the city. In fact, nearly 10 percent of all accidents in the city occur at the corner. This intersection is very dangerous, and a traffic signal should be installed there before a life is lost.

The details in the paragraph progress from least important to most important. They achieve their full effect in the main idea statement at the end.

In many cases, the main idea is not expressed in a single sentence. The reader is called upon to interpret all of the ideas expressed in the paragraph and to decide upon a main idea. Read the following paragraph.

> The American author Jack London was once a pupil at the Cole Grammar School in Oakland, California. Each morning the class sang a song. When the teacher noticed that Jack wouldn't sing, she sent him to the principal. He returned to class with a note. The note said that Jack could be excused from singing with the class if he would write an essay every morning.

In this paragraph, the reader has to interpret the individual ideas and to decide on a main idea. This main idea seems reasonable: Jack London's career as a writer began with a punishment in grammar school.

Understanding the concept of the main idea and knowing how to find it is important. Transferring that understanding to your reading and study is also important.

Working Through a Lesson

Part A

1. **Preview the article.** Locate the timed selection in Part A of the lesson that you are going to read. Wait for your teacher's signal to preview. You will have 20 seconds for previewing. Follow the previewing steps described on page 2.

2. **Read the article.** When your teacher gives you the signal, begin reading. Read carefully so that you will be able to answer questions about what you have read. When you finish reading, look at the board and note your reading time. Write this time at the bottom of the page on the line labeled Reading Time.

3. **Complete the exercises.** Answer the 10 questions that follow the article. There are 5 fact questions and 5 idea questions. Choose the best answer to each question and put an X in that box.

4. **Correct your work.** Use the Answer Key at the back of the book to check your answers. Circle any wrong answer and put an X in the box you should have marked. Record the number of correct answers on the appropriate line at the end of the lesson.

Part B

1. **Preview and read the passage.** Use the same techniques you

used to read Part A. Think about what you are reading.

2. **Complete the exercises.** Instructions are given for answering each category of question. There are 15 responses for you to record.

3. **Correct your work.** Use the Answer Key at the back of the book. Circle any wrong answer and write the correct letter or number next to it. Record the number of correct answers on the appropriate line at the end of the lesson.

Plotting Your Progress

1. **Find your reading rate.** Turn to the Reading Rate graph on page 116. Put an X at the point where the vertical line that represents the lesson intersects your reading time, shown along the left-hand side. The right-hand side of the graph will reveal your words-per-minute reading speed.

2. **Find your comprehension score.** Add your scores for Part A and Part B to determine your total number of correct answers. Turn to the Comprehension Score graph on page 117. Put an X at the point where the vertical line that represents your lesson intersects your total correct answers, shown along the left-hand side. The right-hand side of the graph will show the percentage of questions you answered correctly.

3. **Complete the Comprehension Skills Profile.** Turn to page 118. Record your incorrect answers for the Part B exercises. The five Part B skills are listed along the bottom. There are five columns of boxes, one column for each question. For every incorrect answer, put an X in a box for that skill.

To get the most benefit from these lessons, you need to take charge of your own progress in improving your reading speed and comprehension. Studying these graphs will help you to see whether your reading rate is increasing and to determine what skills you need to work on. Your teacher will also review the graphs to check your progress.

About the Series

Timed Readings Plus in Science includes 10 books at reading levels 4–13, with one book at each level. Book One contains material at a fourth-grade reading level; Book Two at a fifth-grade level, and so on. The readability level is determined by the Fry Readability Scale and is not to be confused with grade or age level. The books are designed for use with students at middle-school level and above.

The purposes of the series are as follows:

- to provide systematic, structured reading practice that helps students improve their reading rate and comprehension skills

- to give students practice in reading and understanding informational articles in the content area of science

- to give students experience in reading various text types—informational, expository, narrative, and prescriptive

- to prepare students for taking standardized tests that include timed reading passages in various content areas

- to provide materials with a wide range of reading levels so that students can continue to practice and improve their reading rate and comprehension skills

Because the books are designed for use with students at designated reading levels rather than in a particular grade, the science topics in this series are not correlated to any grade-level curriculum. Most standardized tests require students to read and comprehend science passages. This series provides an opportunity for students to become familiar with the particular requirements of reading science. For example, the vocabulary in a science article is important. Students need to know certain words in order to understand the concepts and the information.

Each book in the series contains 25 two-part lessons. Part A focuses on improving reading rate. This section of the lesson consists of a 400-word timed informational article on a science topic followed by two multiple-choice exercises. Recalling Facts includes five fact questions; Understanding Ideas includes five critical-thinking questions.

Part B concentrates on building mastery in critical areas of comprehension. This section consists of a nontimed passage—the "plus" passage—followed by five exercises that address five major comprehension skills. The passage varies in length; its subject matter relates to the content of the timed selection.

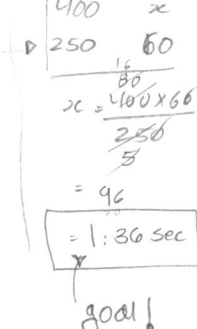

Timed Reading and Comprehension

Timed reading is the best-known method of improving reading speed. There is no point in someone's reading at an accelerated speed if the person does not understand what she or he is reading. Nothing is more important than comprehension in reading. The main purpose of reading is to gain knowledge and insight, to understand the information that the writer and the text are communicating.

Few students will be able to read a passage once and answer all of the questions correctly. A score of 70 or 80 percent correct is normal. If the student gets 90 or 100 percent correct, he or she is either reading too slowly or the material is at too low a reading level. A comprehension or critical thinking score of less than 70 percent indicates a need for improvement.

One method of improving comprehension and critical-thinking skills is for the student to go back and study each incorrect answer. First, the student should reread the question carefully. It is surprising how many students get the wrong answer simply because they have not read the question carefully. Then the student should look back in the passage to find the place where the question is answered, reread that part of the passage, and think about how to arrive at the correct answer. It is important to be able to recognize a correct answer when it is embedded in the text. Teacher guidance or class discussion will help the student find an answer.

Speed Versus Comprehension

It is not unusual for comprehension scores to decline as reading rate increases during the early weeks of timed readings. If this happens, students should attempt to level off their speed—but not lower it—and concentrate more on comprehension. Usually, if students maintain the higher speed and concentrate on comprehension, scores will gradually improve and within a week or two be back up to normal levels of 70 to 80 percent.

It is important to achieve a proper balance between speed and comprehension. An inefficient reader typically reads everything at one speed, usually slowly. Some poor readers, however, read rapidly but without satisfactory comprehension. It is important to achieve a balance between speed and comprehension. The practice that this series provides enables students to increase their reading speed while maintaining normal levels of comprehension.

Getting Started

As a rule, the passages in a book designed to improve reading speed should be relatively easy. The student should not have much difficulty with the vocabulary or the subject matter. Don't worry about the passages being too easy; students should see how quickly and efficiently they can read a passage.

Begin by assigning students to a level. A student should start with a book that is one level below his or her current reading level. If a student's reading level is not known, a suitable starting point would be one or two levels below the student's present grade in school.

Introduce students to the contents and format of the book they are using. Examine the book to see how it is organized. Talk about the parts of each lesson. Discuss the purpose of timed reading and the use of the progress graphs at the back of the book.

Timing the Reading

One suggestion for timing the reading is to have all students begin reading the selection at the same time. After one minute, write on the board the time that has elapsed and begin updating it at 10-second intervals (1:00, 1:10, 1:20, etc.). Another option is to have individual students time themselves with a stopwatch.

Teaching a Lesson

Part A

1. Give students the signal to begin previewing the lesson. Allow 20 seconds, then discuss special science terms or vocabulary that students found.

2. Use one of the methods described above to time students as they read the passage. (Include the 20-second preview time as part of the first minute.) Tell students to write down the last time shown on the board or the stopwatch when they finish reading. Have them record the time in the designated space after the passage.

3. Next, have students complete the exercises in Part A. Work with them to check their answers, using the Answer Key that begins on page 114. Have them circle incorrect answers, mark the correct answers, and then record the numbers of correct answers for Part A on the appropriate line at the end of the lesson. Correct responses to eight or more questions indicate satisfactory comprehension and recall.

Part B

1. Have students read the Part B passage and complete the exercises that follow it. Directions are provided with each exercise. Correct responses require deliberation and discrimination.

2. Work with students to check their answers. Then discuss the answers with them and have them record the number of correct answers for Part B at the end of the lesson.

Have students study the correct answers to the questions they answered incorrectly. It is important that they understand why a particular answer is correct or incorrect.

Have them reread relevant parts of a passage to clarify an answer. An effective cooperative activity is to have students work in pairs to discuss their answers, explain why they chose the answers they did, and try to resolve differences.

Monitoring Progress

Have students find their total correct answers for the lesson and record their reading time and scores on the graphs on pages 116 and 117. Then have them complete the Comprehension Skills Profile on page 118. For each incorrect response to a question in Part B, students should mark an X in the box above each question type.

The legend on the Reading Rate graph automatically converts reading times to words-per-minute rates. The Comprehension Score graph automatically converts the raw scores to percentages.

These graphs provide a visual record of a student's progress. This record gives the student and you an opportunity to evaluate the student's progress and to determine the types of exercises and skills he or she needs to concentrate on.

Diagnosis and Evaluation

The following are typical reading rates.

Slow Reader—150 Words Per Minute

Average Reader—250 Words Per Minute

Fast Reader—350 Words Per Minute

A student who consistently reads at an average or above-average rate (with satisfactory comprehension) is ready to advance to the next book in the series.

A column of Xs in the Comprehension Skills Profile indicates a specific comprehension weakness. Using the profile, you can assess trends in student performance and suggest remedial work if necessary.

In the 1450s Johannes Gutenberg, a German printer, developed a printing press in which individual letters could be arranged in lines to create a page of text. Each letter was cast in metal and could be moved around to different parts of the press depending on which words were needed on a particular page. This use of movable type was one of the most important developments in modern history. Previously, most books had been created by copying out text by hand. It had taken many hours to create a single book. With the Gutenberg press, pages could be created in a matter of seconds, and many copies of books could be created in a few hours. Gutenberg printed a Bible in large quantities, and its distribution throughout Europe had profound social consequences.

Gutenberg's printing press was not so much an invention, however, as an adaptation of evolving technologies. Printing pictures on paper, using carved and inked wooden blocks, had been a well-known artistic technique in China and Japan since the eighth century. European artists were making block prints by the end of the 14th century. Another contribution to Gutenberg's new system also originated in the East: paper. The Chinese invented paper made from rags. Muslim countries were making this inexpensive paper by 800, and it was introduced into Europe in about 1000. Initially an unpopular alternative to writing sheets made from the skins of animals, rag paper was ideal for the new European printing presses, as it absorbed the oily ink required for the metal type.

Printing soon became an important industry in a rapidly growing world. In 1476, William Caxton of London printed and distributed a number of popular stories, including Chaucer's *Canterbury Tales*. By 1500, nearly 35,000 books were in print worldwide. The American colonies acquired their first printing press in 1638 when Stephen and Matthew Daye set up shop in Cambridge, Massachusetts.

The printing press did not change significantly for a long time. In the 19th century, however, iron replaced wood in the press's framework, and paper became available in continuous rolls rather than more expensive single sheets. Steam engines increased the speed at which the presses ran. The introduction of linotype machines meant that printing plates could be created more rapidly. In the late 1900s, the introduction of high-speed offset presses and the integration of computer technology drastically cut the amount of time it took to turn ideas into books.

Reading Time 2 min

Recalling Facts

1. The inventor of movable type was
   - ❏ a. Stephen Daye.
   - ❏ b. Johannes Gutenberg.
   - ❏ c. William Caxton.

2. Which was *not* true of movable type?
   - ❏ a. Movable type was used to print photographs.
   - ❏ b. Individual letters were cast in metal.
   - ❏ c. Letters were arranged in lines.

3. Rag paper was developed in
   - ❏ a. Europe.
   - ❏ b. Muslim countries.
   - ❏ c. China.

4. William Caxton had a particular interest in
   - ❏ a. religious texts.
   - ❏ b. popular stories.
   - ❏ c. political pamphlets.

5. Which was *not* a 19th-century improvement in the printing press?
   - ❏ a. use of steam engines
   - ❏ b. paper on rolls
   - ❏ c. oily printer's ink

Understanding Ideas

6. One could conclude that
   - ❏ a. the printing press made books more widely available.
   - ❏ b. the first printed books cost a great deal of money.
   - ❏ c. the movable-type press came from China.

7. Why might the mass printing of the Gutenberg Bible have had profound social consequences?
   - ❏ a. No Bibles were available prior to that time.
   - ❏ b. For the first time, ordinary people could afford Bibles.
   - ❏ c. The Gutenberg Bible was the first complete Bible.

8. The movable-type printing press was in use for about _____ before being significantly improved.
   - ❏ a. six centuries
   - ❏ b. four centuries
   - ❏ c. ten centuries

9. What has been an ongoing theme in the history of printing?
   - ❏ a. Books have been getting more and more interesting.
   - ❏ b. Books have been made more quickly and less expensively.
   - ❏ c. Well-educated people have benefited the most from advances in printing.

10. The development of the movable-type printing press
   - ❏ a. had little effect on society.
   - ❏ b. depended on the discoveries of many different people.
   - ❏ c. occurred over a three-week period.

The Book and Electronic Publishing

Computer jargon has spawned new terms that at the start of the 21st century had not yet entered standard dictionaries: one of these terms is "e-book." An e-book is any publication that can be downloaded and read on a computer. Tomorrow's library might be a modest building, perhaps only an alcove filled with computer terminals from which patrons can download books onto laptops or handheld electronic devices. No longer would it be necessary to clear forests to produce innumerable reams of paper; no longer would a library dedicate endless lengths of shelving to the storage of its collections.

There is no consensus as to the probable evolution of electronic publishing. What new inventions will ease the distribution of e-books? Can people relinquish the pure experience of the weight of the book, the feel of the pages, and even the smell of ink? Will readers ever be able to flip through the pages of an e-book as easily as they can flip through the pages of a printed book?

In addition to e-book technologies in publishing, there is also the option of print-on-demand technology. Print-on-demand (POD) allows the creation of a single volume of a book, avoiding the expense of mass printings. Publishers might take advantage of e-books and POD technology to introduce new authors; they could also reproduce a book long out of print but still valuable to scholars.

(56 sec) 2nd time

1. **Recognizing Words in Context**

Find the word *relinquish* in the passage. One definition below is closest to the meaning of that word. One definition has the opposite or nearly opposite meaning. The remaining definition has a completely different meaning. Label the definitions C for *closest*, O for *opposite or nearly opposite*, and D for *different*.

_____ a. study

_____ b. give up

_____ c. acquire

2. **Distinguishing Fact from Opinion**

Two of the statements below present *facts*, which can be proved correct. The other statement is an *opinion*, which expresses someone's thoughts or beliefs. Label the statements F for *fact* and O for *opinion*.

_____ a. In the future, libraries should contain only computers instead of traditional books.

_____ b. Electronic publishing includes e-books and other technologies.

_____ c. An e-book can be read using a handheld electronic device.

3. Keeping Events in Order

Label the statements below 1, 2, and 3 to show the order in which the events happen.

_____ a. Libraries need less shelf space and more computer terminals.

_____ b. Libraries need a great deal of shelving space.

_____ c. More books begin appearing in e-book formats than in traditional formats.

4. Making Correct Inferences

Two of the statements below are correct *inferences,* or reasonable guesses. They are based on information in the passage. The other statement is an incorrect, or faulty, inference. Label the statements C for *correct* inference and F for *faulty* inference.

_____ a. High printing costs prevent the publishing of important books that only a few people would buy.

_____ b. Within 20 years, all students will get their textbook lessons from handheld electronic devices.

_____ c. Advances in technology have unclear ramifications for the publishing industry.

5. Understanding Main Ideas

One of the statements below expresses the main idea of the passage. One statement is too general, or too broad. The other explains only part of the passage; it is too narrow. Label the statements M for *main idea,* B for *too broad,* and N for *too narrow.*

_____ a. Advances in computer technology are changing society.

_____ b. E-books require the use of a handheld device.

_____ c. E-books and other technologies are affecting libraries and the publishing industry.

Correct Answers, Part A _6_

Correct Answers, Part B _11_

Total Correct Answers _17_

People use the word *weather* to describe meteorological conditions—temperature, precipitation, humidity, wind, cloudiness, and so on. All of this atmospheric activity brings about change on the ground below. Any kind of contact with air, water, or living matter affects the rock from which Earth was formed more than 4 billion years ago.

Weathering is the process of change in Earth's surface. It includes any kind of decomposition or disintegration. Decomposition is weathering caused by chemical reactions. Disintegration is weathering caused by physical forces. One of the most important byproducts of weathering is the creation of soils and sedimentary rocks.

One kind of chemical weathering is the process called hydrolysis. In an example of hydrolysis, water saturates granite, and the hydrogen in the water interacts with the mineral feldspar to form clay mineral, a crumbling substance that weakens the granite, making erosion possible. Oxidation is another example of chemical weathering. The element iron, for example, combines with the oxygen in water or air to form iron oxide, the reddish-brown material we know as rust. Like clay mineral, iron oxide is friable, or fragile, and can weaken rock.

The friction caused by wind, sand, or water; the weight of ice; or the pressure from roots of lichens, moss, and other plants can cause physical weathering, sometimes called mechanical weathering. Physical weathering involves no chemical reactions but only the breaking up of rock into fragments. When physical weathering results in the movement of mineral particles—a process called mass wasting—it becomes erosion.

Erosion is any natural process that causes the movement of minerals. Through the action of wind, water, ice, and gravity, erosion moves minerals—in essence, fragments of rock—from their original location to a new one. Fast-moving river water, for instance, erodes dirt from its banks and carries it downstream; the particles settle onto the river bottom at points where the current is no longer strong enough to keep them afloat. Sandstorms have scoured rock formations into fantastic shapes. As moisture seeps into cracks and crevices and then freezes, the pressure of its expanding volume can fracture rock and scrape away tiny fragments.

Simply put, if a particle is loosened from a rock by a chemical or mechanical process, but stays put, it is an example of weathering. Once the particle is separated from its source by wind, water, ice, or gravity, it is an example of erosion.

Reading Time _____

Recalling Facts

1. Weathering _____ erosion.
   - ❏ a. is the same as
   - ❏ b. is not the same as
   - ❏ c. comes after

2. Which of the following is *not* an example of chemical weathering?
   - ❏ a. hydrolysis
   - ❏ b. oxidation
   - ❏ c. disintegration

3. Physical weathering refers to
   - ❏ a. the disintegration of rock.
   - ❏ b. the decomposition of rock.
   - ❏ c. chemical changes in rock.

4. Erosion is involved
   - ❏ a. in the fragmention of rock.
   - ❏ b. in the transportation of rock.
   - ❏ c. in the strengthening of rock.

5. Which of the following is a direct cause of erosion?
   - ❏ a. humidity
   - ❏ b. heat
   - ❏ c. gravity

Understanding Ideas

6. If something is friable, it is easily
   - ❏ a. crumbled.
   - ❏ b. bent.
   - ❏ c. dissolved.

7. The presence of soil on Earth
   - ❏ a. depends on the amount of weather in the area.
   - ❏ b. is the result of billions of years of the weathering and erosion of rock.
   - ❏ c. began with the growth of lichens and mosses.

8. One could conclude from this article that Earth
   - ❏ a. has all the soil it will ever have.
   - ❏ b. is unaffected by atmospheric activity.
   - ❏ c. looked rocky and barren when it was first formed.

9. One could conclude from this article that grains of sand
   - ❏ a. started out as solid rock.
   - ❏ b. come from desert areas.
   - ❏ c. were all produced by the action of water.

10. _____ explains how rock that originated in one place might be found many miles away.
    - ❏ a. Hydrolysis
    - ❏ b. Weathering
    - ❏ c. Erosion

Weather Forecasting Through the Ages

The peoples of the earliest civilizations watched the skies and made offerings to their gods in an effort to predict and control the weather. For thousands of years, the power of folklore meant that weather forecasting was rooted more in belief in the supernatural than in science.

As more modern civilizations began to emerge, people began to take a more systematic approach to studying the weather. In the 4th century B.C., the Greek scholar Aristotle created a word to describe the subject of weather: *meteorology.* One of his followers wrote a tome on forecasting called *Book of Signs.* Among the lengthy book's assertions was the claim that a ring around the moon is often followed by rain.

It was not until 1593, however, that the Italian scientist Galileo thought of a way to measure the warmth of the air. His student Evangelista Torricelli believed that the weight of the air could change, and in 1643 he invented the barometer to measure air pressure. Other scientists found ways to measure humidity, wind, and precipitation. In 1714, the German physicist Daniel Fahrenheit invented the modern thermometer.

In the 1800s scientists began to make weather maps to help with forecasting. Computers help today's meteorologists make forecasts that are more accurate than ever before.

(50 sec) 2nd time

1. **Recognizing Words in Context**

   Find the word *tome* in the passage. One definition below is closest to the meaning of that word. One definition has the opposite or nearly opposite meaning. The remaining definition has a completely different meaning. Label the definitions C for *closest,* O for *opposite or nearly opposite,* and D for *different.*

   _____ a. scientific journal

   _____ b. long book

   _____ c. short pamphlet

2. **Distinguishing Fact from Opinion**

   Two of the statements below present *facts,* which can be proved correct. The other statement is an *opinion,* which expresses someone's thoughts or beliefs. Label the statements F for *fact* and O for *opinion.*

   _____ a. The invention of the barometer was the most important event in the history of meteorology.

   _____ b. Computers help today's meteorologists predict the weather.

   _____ c. Early weather forecasting was influenced by people's belief in the supernatural.

3. Keeping Events in Order

Label the statements below 1, 2, and 3 to show the order in which the events happen.

_____ a. Aristotle creates a new branch of science called meteorology.

_____ b. Meteorologists begin making weather maps to help with forecasting.

_____ c. Galileo figures out how to measure temperature.

4. Making Correct Inferences

Two of the statements below are correct *inferences*, or reasonable guesses. They are based on information in the passage. The other statement is an incorrect, or faulty, inference. Label the statements C for *correct* inference and F for *faulty* inference.

_____ a. Early civilizations believed that gods controlled the weather.

_____ b. Computer-generated forecasts have a 99 percent rate of accuracy.

_____ c. Precise measurements of atmospheric conditions help in weather forecasting.

5. Understanding Main Ideas

One of the statements below expresses the main idea of the passage. One statement is too general, or too broad. The other explains only part of the passage; it is too narrow. Label the statements M for *main idea*, B for *too broad*, and N for *too narrow*.

_____ a. Aristotle and Galileo contributed to the development of meteorology.

_____ b. Meteorology is one of the earth sciences.

_____ c. Over time, weather forecasting developed from an attempt to understand the supernatural into a science.

Correct Answers, Part A ___9___

Correct Answers, Part B ___15___

Total Correct Answers ___24___

For centuries, astronomers, physicists, and mathematicians have studied space, time, and gravitation in an effort to better understand the universe. Although scientists do not yet fully understand each of these properties, they have learned a considerable amount about the relationships between them.

The word *space* conjures up an image of a vast universe, but space is also the measurable distance that separates one thing from another. The space between a pencil and a calculator on a desk might measure 20 centimeters (8 inches), and the space between Earth and the Sun can be as much as 150 million kilometers (94 million miles), depending on Earth's position in its orbit. Spatial distance is measured in linear units such as centimeters or miles; astronomical distance is often measured in units of time, such as light years.

Time is the experience of duration, or the period during which an activity is completed. People understand time, for example, as the measurement of history. Time is the distance separating a person from an occurrence in the past or future. Time can be divided into small units, such as minutes and days, or large units, such as centuries and millennia. A star in a different galaxy is light years away from Earth. A light year is the distance that light travels through space in a single year. In astronomical terms, the Sun is comparatively nearby, not even one "light hour" from Earth. Light generated by the Sun reaches Earth in only eight minutes. The star Alpha Centauri, however, is 4.4 light years from Earth, so 4.4 years go by while the star's light travels the more than 40 trillion kilometers (25 trillion miles) to Earth.

Gravitation is the force attracting objects toward each other; it exerts its pull on matter and energy alike. Gravitation keeps the planets in orbit around the Sun, it helps determine the movement of other celestial bodies, and it keeps light from escaping from black holes. Gravitation is strongest, however, when large objects, such as moons, are involved: the larger the object, the greater its gravitational pull. Human beings, for instance, exert a relatively small gravitational pull on each other; the planets and stars, however, are held in their various paths by many different gravitational pulls acting upon them. It is gravity that keeps people attached firmly to the ground and keeps the atmosphere in place so that we can breathe.

Recalling Facts

1. Space is
   - ❏ a. the measurable distance separating objects.
   - ❏ b. a distance that changes depending on the unit of measurement.
   - ❏ c. a vast distance.

2. Time is one's experience of
   - ❏ a. the movement of light through space.
   - ❏ b. a period in which an action is completed.
   - ❏ c. waiting for the future.

3. Gravitation is a force exerted by
   - ❏ a. objects on any other objects.
   - ❏ b. light from the Sun.
   - ❏ c. Earth's atmosphere.

4. Units of both distance and time can be used to measure
   - ❏ a. space.
   - ❏ b. gravitational pull.
   - ❏ c. historical eras.

5. A light year is
   - ❏ a. a distance of 40 trillion kilometers.
   - ❏ b. the time elapsed between light's leaving the Sun and arriving on Earth.
   - ❏ c. the distance light travels through space in one year.

Understanding Ideas

6. One may conclude from the article that
   - ❏ a. scientists have a clear understanding of the workings of the universe.
   - ❏ b. spatial distance can be understood as the passing of time.
   - ❏ c. scientists are concerned only with measuring the universe.

7. Light from the star Alpha Centauri that is visible on Earth
   - ❏ a. is created by the star while it is being observed.
   - ❏ b. is only an illusion; it isn't real.
   - ❏ c. was emitted by the star several years ago.

8. Earth is larger than the Moon, so its gravitational force is _____ that of the Moon.
   - ❏ a. greater than
   - ❏ b. less than
   - ❏ c. about the same as

9. Any object that is a light year away is, in relation to distances on Earth,
   - ❏ a. quite close.
   - ❏ b. far away.
   - ❏ c. in a different universe.

10. One may conclude from this article that since the universe was formed, it has been
    - ❏ a. slowly shrinking.
    - ❏ b. increasing in size.
    - ❏ c. staying the same size.

Albert Einstein

With his shaggy gray hair, baggy sweater, and thick mustache, Albert Einstein is for many people the very picture of genius.

Born to a German-Jewish family in 1879, Einstein did not learn to talk until he was three years old. He followed his interest in mathematics to the Polytechnic Institute in Zurich, Switzerland, where his professors did not regard him as a promising student. In 1902 Einstein accepted a job in the patent office in Bern, Switzerland; it was while working there in obscurity that he made some of his greatest discoveries.

In March 1905, Einstein published a paper describing light as consisting of particles of energy. In May of the same year, he demonstrated that atoms are constantly in motion, proving the widely held theory of Brownian motion. A month later, Einstein proved that the speed of light is unaffected by any kind of motion and called the idea his "special theory of relativity." In September he showed that mass and energy are really the same thing with his equation $E = mc^2$. In 1922, Albert Einstein won the Nobel Prize in physics, not for the special theory of relativity for which he is most famous, but primarily for his discovery of the law of the photoelectric effect. Einstein joined Princeton University in 1932 as a professor and continued to make contributions to the science of physics until his death in 1955.

(50 sec) 4/20

1. **Recognizing Words in Context**

   Find the word *obscurity* in the passage. One definition below is closest to the meaning of that word. One definition has the opposite or nearly opposite meaning. The remaining definition has a completely different meaning. Label the definitions C for *closest*, O for *opposite or nearly opposite*, and D for *different*.

   _____ a. being famous

   _____ b. being busy

   _____ c. being unknown

2. **Distinguishing Fact from Opinion**

   Two of the statements below present *facts*, which can be proved correct. The other statement is an *opinion*, which expresses someone's thoughts or beliefs. Label the statements F for *fact* and O for *opinion*.

   _____ a. Einstein was the greatest genius of modern times.

   _____ b. Einstein wore baggy sweaters.

   _____ c. Einstein influenced many scientists.

3. Keeping Events in Order

Label the statements below 1, 2, and 3 to show the order in which the events happened.

_____ a. Einstein joined the faculty of Princeton University.

_____ b. Einstein won the Nobel Prize in physics.

_____ c. Einstein published his special theory of relativity.

4. Making Correct Inferences

Two of the statements below are correct *inferences*, or reasonable guesses. They are based on information in the passage. The other statement is an incorrect, or faulty, inference. Label the statements C for *correct* inference and F for *faulty* inference.

_____ a. Einstein was reluctant to share his work with others.

_____ b. Einstein did not seem particularly intelligent as a child.

_____ c. Einstein was able to take others' theories and apply them to new areas.

5. Understanding Main Ideas

One of the statements below expresses the main idea of the passage. One statement is too general, or too broad. The other explains only part of the passage; it is too narrow. Label the statements M for *main idea*, B for *too broad*, and N for *too narrow*.

_____ a. Albert Einstein made many key discoveries in physics in the early 1900s.

_____ b. Albert Einstein showed that mass and energy are the same by using the equation $E = mc^2$.

_____ c. The early 20th century was a time of great change in scientific thinking.

Correct Answers, Part A ___8___

Correct Answers, Part B ___15___

Total Correct Answers ___23___

Power and Leadership in the Wolf Pack

Wolves belong to the animal family Canidae, which also includes such animals as the jackal, coyote, fox, and dog. Some of these canids, such as the fox, are solitary hunters and raise their young alone; wolves, however, are regarded as social animals, living in well-organized packs of 8 to 20 or more animals. A pack generally includes only one breeding pair and their offspring, but occasionally it may include one or two unrelated wolves. Occasionally, different packs join together during difficult times, such as harsh winters, to find and bring down large game.

The cooperative nature of these packs is remarkable. Raising the pups, for instance, is a collective responsibility. Adult wolves in the pack may bring food to the mother while she is nursing; later they will feed the growing pups on partly digested food they have regurgitated. Various adult wolves watch over the young ones, protecting them, playing with them, and teaching them to hunt.

Wolves, which usually live in northern forests, often search for food with all other wolves in the pack, working collectively to bring down large animals such as caribou and elk. Each pack usually has its own territory for hunting. Wolves are protective of these territories, and they sometimes kill other wolves that trespass. When members of a pack are separated, vocalizations—including howling, yelping, and growling—help them communicate across long distances, stay in touch during hunting forays, and defend their territory.

Each wolf occupies a particular place in the hierarchy of the pack, in which high-ranking, powerful wolves—called dominant wolves—govern the weaker, subordinate wolves. The leading male wolf is often designated the alpha male, and the leading female is the alpha female. When a dominant member of the pack encounters a subordinate one, the dominant wolf stands erect, holding its tail high and its ears forward; it may also growl or bare its teeth. The subordinate wolf, in contrast, crouches down, lowers its tail between its legs, and flattens its ears; it may whine as well. It is possible that this cringing, submissive posture may play an important role in creating emotional bonds between wolves.

According to current studies, the alpha pair in a wolf pack is the only breeding pair. Alpha status in a wolf pack is rarely permanent, however. New research suggests that as younger wolves pair off, they assume the alpha roles, and animals no longer breeding cede their alpha status.

Reading Time _1:45_ (6/20)

Recalling Facts

1. Wolves belong to the family Canidae, which does *not* include
   - ❏ a. coyotes.
   - ❏ b. cougars.
   - ❏ c. jackals.

2. A wolf pack always includes
   - ❏ a. one breeding pair of wolves.
   - ❏ b. several breeding pairs of wolves.
   - ❏ c. at least 20 wolves.

3. Alpha wolves are considered to be the
   - ❏ a. dominant wolves.
   - ❏ b. subordinate wolves.
   - ❏ c. most intelligent wolves.

4. Wolves hunt in packs
   - ❏ a. because they are timid by nature.
   - ❏ b. in order to frighten off other wolves.
   - ❏ c. in order to bring down large prey.

5. Wolf pups are cared for
   - ❏ a. only by the alpha female wolf.
   - ❏ b. by all the adult wolves in the pack.
   - ❏ c. only by the alpha male wolf.

Understanding Ideas

6. One may conclude from this article that the main purpose of a wolf pack is
   - ❏ a. determining which wolves will be alpha females.
   - ❏ b. hunting prey.
   - ❏ c. preventing attacks by predators.

7. Submissive behavior on the part of one wolf toward another suggests that
   - ❏ a. old wolves are frightened of younger wolves.
   - ❏ b. wolves are unpredictable animals that often change packs.
   - ❏ c. wolves in a pack develop well-defined relationships.

8. According to the information in the article, you would be most likely to find wolves in
   - ❏ a. Canada.
   - ❏ b. Brazil.
   - ❏ c. Italy.

9. Like humans, wolves
   - ❏ a. use logic in making decisions.
   - ❏ b. eat meat and plants.
   - ❏ c. live in family groups.

10. For wolves, howling is primarily a way of
    - ❏ a. expressing emotion.
    - ❏ b. communicating with other wolves.
    - ❏ c. scaring off humans.

The Mysterious Nature of Wolves

The wolf is a prominent figure in cultural traditions around the world, but some cultures view wolves differently than other cultures do. Some peoples view wolves as cruel and cunning, while others see them as cowardly. Although frequently a symbol of darkness and evil, the wolf is also associated with light and the sun. The wolf has a reputation for savage and ferocious behavior, yet it can also demonstrate nurturing, caring qualities.

In ancient Greece, even though the wolf was identified with the sun god, Apollo, it also represented danger, as in Aesop's fable "The Boy Who Cried Wolf." More than 2,500 years ago, the Romans made the wolf a symbol of maternal care because, according to legend, a she-wolf raised Romulus, the mythical hero who founded Rome, and his twin brother Remus. On the other hand, the wolf was also associated with Mars, the Roman god of war. In Asia, Genghis Khan, the 13th-century conqueror, claimed to be descended from a blue-gray wolf born of the sky.

In stories collected from various Native American groups during the past hundred years, the wolf represents loyalty, success, perseverance, and intelligence. The Zuni tribe held that the wolf symbolized the east, the direction of the rising sun. The Pawnee and the Ute made the wolf a central figure of their creation stories. Wolves are often pathfinders and teachers in Native American lore but are sometimes forces of evil as well.

1. Recognizing Words in Context

Find the word *nurturing* in the passage. One definition below is closest to the meaning of that word. One definition has the opposite or nearly opposite meaning. The remaining definition has a completely different meaning. Label the definitions C for *closest*, O for *opposite or nearly opposite*, and D for *different*.

_____ a. helping

_____ b. attacking

_____ c. howling

2. Distinguishing Fact from Opinion

Two of the statements below present *facts*, which can be proved correct. The other statement is an *opinion*, which expresses someone's thoughts or beliefs. Label the statements F for *fact* and O for *opinion*.

_____ a. The wolf has roles in cultural traditions around the world.

_____ b. Wolves are a menace because they kill valuable livestock.

_____ c. The wolf has been an important figure for several Native American groups.

3. Keeping Events in Order

Label the statements below 1, 2, and 3 to show the order in which the events happened.

_____ a. Genghis Khan claimed he was descended from a wolf.

_____ b. Wolf stories from Native American cultures were collected.

_____ c. The Romans viewed the wolf as a symbol of maternal care.

4. Making Correct Inferences

Two of the statements below are correct *inferences,* or reasonable guesses. They are based on information in the passage. The other statement is an incorrect, or faulty, inference. Label the statements C for *correct* inference and F for *faulty* inference.

_____ a. Wolves live in countries in all parts of the world.

_____ b. Wolf behavior can suggest both positive and negative qualities.

_____ c. People have observed wolves for thousands of years.

5. Understanding Main Ideas

One of the statements below expresses the main idea of the passage. One statement is too general, or too broad. The other explains only part of the passage; it is too narrow. Label the statements M for *main idea,* B for *too broad,* and N for *too narrow.*

_____ a. Legends concerning animals are important in many cultures.

_____ b. Wolves are closely linked to ideas about light and the sun.

_____ c. Wolves are viewed differently by various ethnic groups.

Correct Answers, Part A ___7___

Correct Answers, Part B ___15___

Total Correct Answers ___22___

Producers and Consumers: The Food Chain

In 1927, a scientist named Charles Elton developed the concept of the food chain to describe the interdependency of all organisms within an ecosystem.

Living things that create their own food, such as green plants, are called autotrophs. They are the first link in the food chain because they capture the sun's energy and use it to convert inorganic compounds, such as minerals, into energy-rich organic compounds such as sugars and proteins. Living things that create their own food are sometimes called producers.

Above producers in food chains are the heterotrophs, sometimes called consumers, which depend on other organisms for food. Herbivores are considered first-level consumers: they are animals that eat only plants. Carnivores—animals that eat only meat—are second-level consumers. Food chains track the amount of energy transferred as nutrients from one organism to another within an ecosystem. Food chains demonstrate that the survival of all life forms in an ecosystem depends on the success of all the others.

The expression "food chain," however, is misleading as a metaphor. It is true that a field of thick grass, full of sugars and proteins produced using energy from sunlight, provides nutritional energy for a colony of rabbits that in turn become an energy source for foxes. In this example, foxes are at the top of the food chain. If there is an infestation of grasshoppers or a drought that destroys the grass, then the number of rabbits declines, bringing about a reduction in the population of foxes.

Yet no group of feeding relationships is this simple, and scientists illustrate these more complicated relationships as food webs. Food webs can be envisioned as a number of food chains linked together. Many different creatures depend on grass for food. Also, rabbits eat a wide variety of plants in addition to grass; foxes will eat almost any small animal, including insects, worms, mice, and fish, as well as eggs and carrion. Changes or problems in the food supply at any level can have widespread effects.

A food web does not have a single dominant species at the top; it is a regenerative cycle, and in addition to producers and consumers, it also includes decomposers. Decomposers are organisms such as bacteria that survive by removing the chemical energy from dead plants and animals and from waste material. This energy is returned to the earth in the form of nutrients and can be used again by vegetation.

Reading Time 1:50 min (6/21)

Recalling Facts

1. A food chain tracks
   - ❏ a. the energy transferred as nutrients in an ecosystem.
   - ❏ b. the number of species in an ecosystem.
   - ❏ c. the variety of plants in an ecosystem.

2. An organism that creates its own food is *not* called
   - ❏ a. an autotroph.
   - ❏ b. a producer.
   - ❏ c. a heterotroph.

3. Green plants convert the sun's energy into
   - ❏ a. inorganic compounds.
   - ❏ b. organic compounds.
   - ❏ c. minerals.

4. Both carnivores and herbivores are called
   - ❏ a. consumers.
   - ❏ b. producers.
   - ❏ c. autotrophs.

5. Decomposers are organisms such as _____ that remove _____ from dead organisms.
   - ❏ a. bacteria; minerals
   - ❏ b. plants; chemical energy
   - ❏ c. bacteria; chemical energy

Understanding Ideas

6. A carnivore would be most likely to eat
   - ❏ a. insects.
   - ❏ b. wheat.
   - ❏ c. mushrooms.

7. Which of the following might *best* represent feeding relationships?
   - ❏ a. a single straight arrow
   - ❏ b. a web of arrows
   - ❏ c. two arrows pointing in different directions

8. One could conclude from this article that
   - ❏ a. all organisms need energy in order to grow and survive.
   - ❏ b. some organisms do not require energy in order to grow and survive.
   - ❏ c. inorganic compounds such as minerals are a source of energy.

9. One could conclude from this article that decomposers
   - ❏ a. are large organisms.
   - ❏ b. are a kind of animal.
   - ❏ c. are tiny organisms.

10. One could conclude from this article that in an ecosystem
    - ❏ a. lower-level consumers are the least important organisms.
    - ❏ b. each organism contributes indirectly to the survival of all organisms.
    - ❏ c. the function of one species can be taken over by many other species.

Nature's Pesticides

The garden is growing beautifully: crimson, coral, and yellow rosebuds are emerging above glossy foliage, green tomatoes decorate plants that are almost four feet tall, and cucumber vines are heavy with sausage-shaped fruit. Suddenly one morning, leaves are discolored and speckled with holes, whole branches are breaking off from primary stems, and the gardener's visions of fragrant bouquets and delicious salads are evaporating. Is it time to drench the backyard in chemical pesticides? Maybe not.

To be healthy and free of noxious pests such as borers, aphids, mites, slugs, and snails, a garden requires a variety of beneficial insect and animal life. Wriggling earthworms aerate the soil and help break down nutrients for the plants to use. Toads, garter snakes, birds, and bats feed on the insects that damage vegetables. Spiders, ladybugs, praying mantises, aphid lions, and ground beetles also eradicate some of the most destructive pests from the garden.

Chemical pesticides are effective at eliminating infestations, but they are indiscriminate—they don't just kill bad bugs, they kill all bugs. Pesticides can get into the soils and harm earthworms; they can have adverse effects on the health of your local wildlife; and they can endanger human health if they are not cleaned thoroughly from fruits and vegetables. If you can determine which pest is doing serious damage to your garden, you may be able to purchase insects that will eat the pests that are damaging your garden.

(1/15)

1. **Recognizing Words in Context**

   Find the word *indiscriminate* in the passage. One definition below is closest to the meaning of that word. One definition has the opposite or nearly opposite meaning. The remaining definition has a completely different meaning. Label the definitions C for *closest,* O for *opposite or nearly opposite,* and D for *different.*

   _____ a. selective

   _____ b. permanent

   _____ c. random

2. **Distinguishing Fact from Opinion**

   Two of the statements below present *facts,* which can be proved correct. The other statement is an *opinion,* which expresses someone's thoughts or beliefs. Label the statements F for *fact* and O for *opinion.*

   _____ a. Borers, mites, and slugs often damage plants in gardens.

   _____ b. Chemical pesticides kill many types of bugs quickly.

   _____ c. Chemical pesticides are a good way to protect a garden.

3. Keeping Events in Order

Label the statements below 1, 2, and 3 to show the order in which the events happen.

_____ a. A gardener carefully searches the garden and finds aphids on rose leaves.

_____ b. Several kinds of flowers begin to wilt in the garden.

_____ c. A gardener purchases ladybugs, which eat aphids.

4. Making Correct Inferences

Two of the statements below are correct *inferences,* or reasonable guesses. They are based on information in the passage. The other statement is an incorrect, or faulty, inference. Label the statements C for *correct* inference and F for *faulty* inference.

_____ a. Adding certain insects to a garden can protect plants.

_____ b. Alternatives to pesticides are available for every type of garden pest.

_____ c. Many bugs are vulnerable to the same types of chemical poisons.

5. Understanding Main Ideas

One of the statements below expresses the main idea of the passage. One statement is too general, or too broad. The other explains only part of the passage; it is too narrow. Label the statements M for *main idea,* B for *too broad,* and N for *too narrow.*

_____ a. Certain insects eat pests that damage gardens.

_____ b. Chemical pesticides can do both harm and good in a garden.

_____ c. Insects eat many types of beneficial plants.

Correct Answers, Part A ___9___

Correct Answers, Part B _____

Total Correct Answers _____

What Is Stress?

Stress, in its simplest definition, is strain caused by some type of force. Today, the word *stress* is used most often when discussing mental health. In this context, stress describes the condition that results from ongoing and unpleasant physical, emotional, or environmental forces. Such forces may include too much work, a tragic event, or air pollution. The forces may cause pain, tension, fear, grief, or anxiety. These discomforts can disturb the body's ability to maintain its normal internal balance. Some level of discomfort is, of course, normal. The occasional presence of pain or anxiety is not by itself a symptom of a serious problem. When such distress is continuous—when the brain and the rest of the body cannot make the adjustments that return a person to his or her normal condition of balance— then we say that the person is suffering from stress.

Although stress itself is usually not considered a disease, studies suggest that it is linked to disease. A growing body of research data connects the risk of heart disease, for instance, to stress within the workplace, the family, and other parts of society. Character traits—such as a tendency to worry, to strive for perfection, or to be competitive—also seem to contribute to stress. It is unclear, however, whether stress itself causes disease. People's responses to stress sometimes put them at risk. For example, a person might respond to stress by eating too much or smoking.

Research conducted in California seems to illustrate that men who report stress from their jobs are more likely than less-stressed men to have plaque building up in the arteries that supply blood to the brain. High levels of this plaque increase a person's chances of having a stroke. The same study, however, did not find any link between stress and arterial plaque in women. Doctors speculate that female hormones may operate in some protective way.

Another study seems to confirm the claims of people with the degenerative neurological disease multiple sclerosis (MS) that stress makes their disease worse. Through the use of magnetic resonance imaging (MRI) brain scans, researchers linked periods of stress in the subjects' lives with evidence of MS disease activity. Researchers also determined that major stressful events were related to the development of new brain lesions.

Stress has also been linked to hypertension, depression, obesity, arthritis, gastrointestinal disorders, skin diseases, and some types of cancer.

Reading Time 1:45

Recalling Facts

1. Stress is *not*
   - ❏ a. a response to long-term problems.
   - ❏ b. an adjustment that returns one's body to a state of balance.
   - ❏ c. strain caused by an unpleasant situation.

2. Stress may not be a disease, but it may be _____ disease.
   - ❏ a. a treatment of
   - ❏ b. a demonstration of
   - ❏ c. linked to

3. The buildup of plaque in arteries leading to the brain is associated with stress in
   - ❏ a. men.
   - ❏ b. women.
   - ❏ c. children.

4. Stress appears to _____ the symptoms of some nerve diseases.
   - ❏ a. eliminate
   - ❏ b. lessen
   - ❏ c. worsen

5. There may be a link between personality traits like _____ and the level of stress a person experiences.
   - ❏ a. perfectionism and competitiveness
   - ❏ b. a tendency to criticize others
   - ❏ c. shyness and sensitivity

Understanding Ideas

6. From the information in the article, one can conclude that a person with very high stress levels is most likely to
   - ❏ a. be overweight.
   - ❏ b. become ill.
   - ❏ c. dislike his or her job.

7. One can conclude from this article that
   - ❏ a. emotional stresses cause mental disorders.
   - ❏ b. most people experience stress at some time.
   - ❏ c. stress shortens a person's life span.

8. People do not experience stress if
   - ❏ a. they eat a healthy diet and get enough sleep.
   - ❏ b. they are highly intelligent.
   - ❏ c. their brains and bodies are able to adjust to difficult circumstances.

9. One can conclude that men and women
   - ❏ a. experience stress differently.
   - ❏ b. do not always have the same level of vulnerability to disease.
   - ❏ c. do not experience stress from the same types of causes.

10. A chronic disease such as multiple sclerosis can probably be regarded as
    - ❏ a. a means to reduce stress.
    - ❏ b. the result of severe personal stress.
    - ❏ c. being aggravated by stress.

Stress Management

Lucia's boss is a tyrant, her car's transmission has disintegrated on the day the rent is due, her fourth-grader has chicken pox, and her elderly parents are having difficulty living on their own; there is nothing *but* stress in her life. What can she do? Stress management is a collection of techniques and treatments that can be used to help reduce and control the level of stress.

Some experts suggest that exercise is a good way to manage stress. Individual aerobic activities, such as running, cycling, and swimming, can help to reduce anxiety and improve the body's ability to handle difficult situations. Competitive activities, such as tennis or a game of one-on-one basketball, often are not as effective at reducing stress.

Breathing is often the key to stress management. In stressful situations, muscles can tense up, and breathing can become shallow and rapid. Taking slow, deep breaths and exhaling fully is likely to restore a measure of calm, at least for the moment. Studies have shown that the breathing exercises used in meditation lead to a stronger sense of self, reductions in anxiety and tension, and improved interpersonal and professional coping skills. Medical studies also have shown that meditation helps with the normalization of blood pressure and improved heart function. In one project, students who regularly practiced some form of meditation showed a significant increase in both math and reading scores.

(50 sec)

1. **Recognizing Words in Context**

Find the word *tyrant* in the passage. One definition below is closest to the meaning of that word. One definition has the opposite or nearly opposite meaning. The remaining definition has a completely different meaning. Label the definitions C for *closest*, O for *opposite or nearly opposite*, and D for *different*.

_____ a. a successful manager

_____ b. a harsh leader

_____ c. an understanding friend

2. **Distinguishing Fact from Opinion**

Two of the statements below present *facts*, which can be proved correct. The other statement is an *opinion*, which expresses someone's thoughts or beliefs. Label the statements F for *fact* and O for *opinion*.

_____ a. Stress can cause rapid, shallow breathing.

_____ b. Vigorous exercise is the best cure for stress.

_____ c. Studies have attributed a number of health benefits to meditation.

3. Keeping Events in Order

Two of the statements below describe events that happen at the same time. The other statement describes an event that happens before or after those events. Label them S for *same time*, B for *before*, or A for *after*.

_____ a. A person practices breathing exercises.

_____ b. A doctor notes a decrease in blood pressure.

_____ c. A person bicycles to work each day.

4. Making Correct Inferences

Two of the statements below are correct *inferences*, or reasonable guesses. They are based on information in the passage. The other statement is an incorrect, or faulty, inference. Label the statements C for *correct* inference and F for *faulty* inference.

_____ a. Playing football is one of the best ways to reduce stress.

_____ b. As stress builds up in life, one can take steps to deal with it.

_____ c. A person does not have to leave the workplace in order to deal with stress.

5. Understanding Main Ideas

One of the statements below expresses the main idea of the passage. One statement is too general, or too broad. The other explains only part of the passage; it is too narrow. Label the statements M for *main idea*, B for *too broad*, and N for *too narrow*.

_____ a. Stress affects people in different ways.

_____ b. There are different ways to reduce and manage the stress in one's life.

_____ c. Breathing exercises can improve both one's health and academic success.

Correct Answers, Part A ___9___

Correct Answers, Part B ___15___

Total Correct Answers ___24___

Air and Water Pollution

Since the 18th century, air and water pollution have been by-products of rapid industrial development. Although this industrial development has been confined to certain areas of the world, pollution affects more areas than just those in which it is created.

About 74 percent of Earth's surface is covered by water, but only 3 percent of its water is classified as freshwater; the rest is salt water. Glaciers and polar ice caps contain about 77 percent of Earth's freshwater. Land-dwelling species—including humans—must survive on what is left. About 22 percent of the freshwater supply is stored underground, and 1 percent appears on the surface as lakes, rivers, and wetlands.

Many pollutants threaten these limited water resources. Although pesticides and fertilizers help farmers grow huge amounts of food in some parts of the world, these chemicals also seep into the ground and sometimes make their way into lakes and rivers. These substances, called runoff, can make water dangerous for people to use. They can upset the chemical balance of a body of water as well, altering its ecology and harming plants and animals. Accidental chemical spills, improperly stored by-products of manufacturing processes, and even household wastes can contaminate groundwater, marshes, and streams. Sometimes the source of water pollution is not determined until much damage has been done.

Acid rain, global warming, and holes in the ozone layer have been linked to air pollution. Power plants and factories that burn fossil fuels such as coal, oil, and natural gas give off sulfur dioxide and nitrogen oxides. These gases combine with water vapor and form acid rain. Acid rain changes the chemistry of soils and bodies of water and has led to the decline of the red spruce and sugar maple forests in northeastern North America. It also has damaged historic stone structures in Europe.

Global warming may be the result of the "greenhouse effect." The burning of fossil fuels increases the levels of gases in the atmosphere that trap the sun's heat. Cutting down forests also contributes to the problem, because trees take in carbon dioxide, a heat-retaining gas, and emit oxygen.

Holes in the ozone layer are in part a result of chemicals such as chlorofluorocarbons (CFCs) that have been used in refrigerators and air conditioners, as solvents, and in spray cans. In recent decades, CFCs have been banned in many countries and replaced by less damaging products.

Reading Time _____

Recalling Facts

1. About _____ of Earth's freshwater is stored underground.
   - ❏ a. 74 percent
   - ❏ b. 77 percent
   - ❏ c. 22 percent

2. Which of the following is *not* true?
   - ❏ a. Freshwater supplies are safe from contamination by household wastes.
   - ❏ b. Pesticides can get into a water supply, making it unfit to drink.
   - ❏ c. Fertilizer runoff from farms can upset the chemical balance of water.

3. _____ has been linked to the decline of red spruce forests in North America.
   - ❏ a. Thinning of the ozone layer
   - ❏ b. Acid rain
   - ❏ c. Global warming

4. One possible cause of global warming is
   - ❏ a. fertilizer in the water supply.
   - ❏ b. acid rain.
   - ❏ c. the burning of natural gas.

5. Chlorofluorocarbons (CFCs)
   - ❏ a. are used in power plants.
   - ❏ b. have been used in air conditioners.
   - ❏ c. are common pesticides.

Understanding Ideas

6. One can conclude that
   - ❏ a. it is up to governments to stop pollution.
   - ❏ b. pollution is primarily a local problem.
   - ❏ c. continued industrial development means continued pollution.

7. The world's increasing population
   - ❏ a. makes it harder to keep air and water supplies clean.
   - ❏ b. is a problem only in cities.
   - ❏ c. creates a greater demand for food than it does for clean water.

8. One can conclude that
   - ❏ a. waste products are not a hazard when stored away from lakes and streams.
   - ❏ b. the contamination of groundwater endangers the freshwater supply.
   - ❏ c. water pollution is primarily a problem in agricultural areas.

9. One can conclude that
   - ❏ a. planting trees can improve the quality of the air.
   - ❏ b. factories are responsible for all air pollution.
   - ❏ c. global warming is the result of holes in the ozone layer.

10. One can conclude that
    - ❏ a. Earth's environment cannot be saved.
    - ❏ b. pesticides and fertilizers should be made illegal.
    - ❏ c. there are steps that can be taken to reduce pollution.

Rachel Carson, Scientist and Writer

Rachel Carson, born in rural Pennsylvania in 1907, had a significant impact on the environment. Carson earned a master's degree in zoology in 1932. It was as a writer and not as a research scientist, however, that she made her mark, sharing her view that human beings are just one element in a larger natural order.

In the articles on natural history Carson wrote for various publications, she expressed dry facts in poetic and persuasive language. She wrote five books. Two of them, *The Sea Around Us* and *The Edge of the Sea,* have been called "biographies of the ocean."

Carson also made the world aware of how scientific discoveries can harm as well as help living things. In her best-selling book *Silent Spring,* Carson challenged the profligate use of chemical pesticides by large agricultural and government organizations. She was the first to detail how the pesticide DDT had entered the food chain and damaged populations of bald eagles, falcons, and brown pelicans by causing the shells of their eggs to become so thin that they could not withstand the weight of the parent bird.

Carson died of cancer in 1964. Today, the Rachel Carson Council collects and disseminates information on pesticide-related issues. In 1970, the Rachel Carson Wildlife Refuge, a large area of salt marsh and freshwater habitat in Maine, was dedicated to her memory.

1. **Recognizing Words in Context**

Find the word *profligate* in the passage. One definition below is closest to the meaning of that word. One definition has the opposite or nearly opposite meaning. The remaining definition has a completely different meaning. Label the definitions C for *closest,* O for *opposite or nearly opposite,* and D for *different.*

_____ a. excessive

_____ b. inadequate

_____ c. authoritative

2. **Distinguishing Fact from Opinion**

Two of the statements below present *facts,* which can be proved correct. The other statement is an *opinion,* which expresses someone's thoughts or beliefs. Label the statements F for *fact* and O for *opinion.*

_____ a. Carson wrote about the natural world.

_____ b. Carson was an insightful person who showed that each of us can make a difference in the world.

_____ c. DDT caused a decline in the population of many birds.

3. Keeping Events in Order

Label the statements below 1, 2, and 3 to show the order in which the events happened.

_____ a. Rachel Carson wrote *Silent Spring*.

_____ b. People began to use DDT to control harmful insects.

_____ c. Eagles and falcons began to lay very thin-shelled eggs.

4. Making Correct Inferences

Two of the statements below are correct *inferences*, or reasonable guesses. They are based on information in the passage. The other statement is an incorrect, or faulty, inference. Label the statements C for *correct* inference and F for *faulty* inference.

_____ a. Carson wrote books that the average person could understand.

_____ b. Dangerous properties of new chemical products may not be immediately apparent.

_____ c. If not for Carson, no one would have learned about the dangers of DDT.

5. Understanding Main Ideas

One of the statements below expresses the main idea of the passage. One statement is too general, or too broad. The other explains only part of the passage; it is too narrow. Label the statements M for *main idea*, B for *too broad*, and N for *too narrow*.

_____ a. Writers have played an important role in the battle against pollution.

_____ b. The scientist Rachel Carson taught people about environmental issues through her writing.

_____ c. Carson's book *Silent Spring* changed the way some pesticides were used.

Correct Answers, Part A 9

Correct Answers, Part B 15

Total Correct Answers 24

Although the scientific method is not the only means of discovering truths about the natural world, it is widely accepted as a valid process for answering questions and solving problems. The scientific method provides clear and systematic steps for using experiments to prove or disprove a hypothesis and reach some conclusion. Some authorities claim that there are four steps; some others claim there are five. There is some disagreement as to whether articulating a conclusion can properly be described as a step. For the purposes of this discussion, however, the method involves a series of five steps.

The first step of the scientific method is the recognition of some phenomenon and the articulation of a question about it such as, What is this? Why does this happen? A phenomenon is anything that can be sensed or experienced; it may also be something that is suggested by common sense, even though it cannot be perceived directly.

Step two is observation: a person collects data that concerns the subject in question and organizes the data. The information that the person collects, combined with facts already known, leads to the formulation of a hypothesis, the third step. A hypothesis is an informed guess and reasonable explanation for the question posed in step one, and it must undergo testing in a fourth step. This testing is usually in the form of experiments that must be objective and take into account as many variables as possible. Precise measurements and control over the circumstances under which experiments are carried out is a standard feature of testing. The experiments are generally repeated to ensure that results are consistent and reproducible.

Once the results have been tabulated and interpreted, the researcher should draw a conclusion as the final step. The conclusion may verify the hypothesis; it may also modify it or disprove it. If a conclusion is to be widely accepted, subsequent related experiments must produce similar or consistent results.

The scientific method might seem to be a straight road to discovery. Often, however, it is a twisting path filled with dead ends, U-turns, and detours. Different hypotheses may predict the same results but for different and even contradictory reasons. Likewise, researchers may have different interpretations of the same data. Within the realm of research, there is always ample opportunity for imagination. The scientific method creates a common language for researchers everywhere, helping the scientific community to bring new knowledge into the world.

Reading Time _1:50_

Recalling Facts

1. The scientific method involves
   - ❑ a. the collection of random observations.
   - ❑ b. the systematic use of experiments.
   - ❑ c. 10 specific steps of discovery and demonstration.

2. Scientists repeat their tests
   - ❑ a. to imitate the work of other scientists.
   - ❑ b. to make sure the results are consistent.
   - ❑ c. because each test has to have different results.

3. A hypothesis is
   - ❑ a. a conclusion reached after the completion of an experiment.
   - ❑ b. a type of experiment.
   - ❑ c. a reasonable explanation of a phenomenon.

4. Which of the following groups of steps is in the correct order?
   - ❑ a. hypothesis, testing, conclusion
   - ❑ b. observation, testing, hypothesis
   - ❑ c. testing, observation, conclusion

5. Which of the following is *not* a true statement?
   - ❑ a. Scientists will always develop identical hypotheses given the same observations.
   - ❑ b. Scientists may come to different conclusions given the same test results.
   - ❑ c. Scientists may use different hypotheses to explain the same phenomenon.

Understanding Ideas

6. One could conclude that
   - ❑ a. the scientific method is the only approved research method.
   - ❑ b. most scientists agree on the value of the scientific method.
   - ❑ c. scientists prefer to develop their own research methods.

7. One could conclude that
   - ❑ a. most scientists are distrustful of research conducted by imaginative people.
   - ❑ b. scientists rely mainly on their creativity and imagination when testing hypotheses.
   - ❑ c. imagination may help a scientist form a hypothesis.

8. Which of the following is true?
   - ❑ a. The same facts may suggest different things to different scientists.
   - ❑ b. Scientists learn the most from a hypothesis they prove to be true.
   - ❑ c. Scientists try to make the results of their experiments agree with their hypotheses.

9. A hypothesis about a phenomenon
   - ❑ a. mostly requires imagination.
   - ❑ b. is shaped by known facts and by observations.
   - ❑ c. is likely to be true.

10. Which of these is *not* likely to be true of good scientists?
    - ❑ a. They work carefully and keep accurate records.
    - ❑ b. They are observant and quick to notice similarities.
    - ❑ c. They use traditional knowledge and reject hypotheses that have never been used.

Following its invention in the 1830s, photography has played a key role in science as well as in art. Scientists have often used photography to observe and analyze forms and to record changes that occur over time. The special value of photography lies in film's ability to record what the human eye cannot. A single photograph provides a wealth of detail, but the eye focuses on one part of a scene—usually what is biggest or brightest. Light-sensitive film can show action that otherwise would be only a blur.

In 1877, Eadweard Muybridge proved that all four of a galloping horse's legs are, at certain points, off the ground at the same time. As a horse galloped past a series of cameras aimed at a calibrated backdrop, it tripped the camera shutters. Each photograph showed a different phase of movement against lines that measured the distance the horse had traveled. In the 1880s Muybridge made many studies of human and animal locomotion. He recorded the movements of different sports and the unique gaits of camels, deer, lions and sloths. He even photographed a cockatoo in flight.

In 1931, Dr. Harold Edgerton, a professor at the Massachusetts Institute of Technology, ushered in ultra-high speed photography when he invented a rapidly flashing light called a strobe. Over the next 40 years, he used it to capture images of motion, including wires snapping, a balloon popping, and milk droplets splashing.

1. **Recognizing Words in Context**

   Find the word *calibrated* in the passage. One definition below is closest to the meaning of that word. One definition has the opposite or nearly opposite meaning. The remaining definition has a completely different meaning. Label the definitions C for *closest*, O for *opposite or nearly opposite*, and D for *different*.

   _____ a. unmeasured and random

   _____ b. brightly colored

   _____ c. systematically measured

2. **Distinguishing Fact from Opinion**

   Two of the statements below present *facts*, which can be proved correct. The other statement is an *opinion*, which expresses someone's thoughts or beliefs. Label the statements F for *fact* and O for *opinion*.

   _____ a. Cameras have provided the most important scientific information.

   _____ b. Scientists have used photography ever since it was invented.

   _____ c. The strobe light made it possible to photograph movement that is too fast to be seen.

3. Keeping Events in Order

Label the statements below 1, 2, and 3 to show the order in which the events happened.

_____ a. Edgerton photographed things that happened too fast for the eye to see.

_____ b. Muybridge documented the movement of a galloping horse.

_____ c. Muybridge published books on animal locomotion.

4. Making Correct Inferences

Two of the statements below are correct *inferences,* or reasonable guesses. They are based on information in the passage. The other statement is an incorrect, or faulty, inference. Label the statements C for *correct* inference and F for *faulty* inference.

_____ a. Photographs can record more information about a scene than the human eye can.

_____ b. The human eye cannot record still images from a figure in motion.

_____ c. Photographers who work with scientists should have an advanced degree in science.

5. Understanding Main Ideas

One of the statements below expresses the main idea of the passage. One statement is too general, or too broad. The other explains only part of the passage; it is too narrow. Label the statements M for *main idea,* B for *too broad,* and N for *too narrow.*

_____ a. Photography has contributed to the study of objects in motion.

_____ b. Photography has made valuable contributions to many fields.

_____ c. Scientists use strobe lights to photograph objects moving at ultra-high speeds.

Correct Answers, Part A _____

Correct Answers, Part B _____

Total Correct Answers _____

The Sounds of Music

Sound is a pressure disturbance moving through air; it is also the auditory perception of that disturbance. Thousands of years ago, scholars compared sound to waves in the ocean and determined that pitch was probably a matter of vibration, or the speed at which a "wave" moved. The Greek mathematician Pythagoras realized that the relationship between certain pitches was particularly pleasant to the human ear and attempted to codify these relationships. By the Middle Ages, harmony—the sound of two or more musical notes played simultaneously—was assigned to the study of mathematics. Scientists proved conclusively during the 17th century that a vibrating body producing a single note causes the air around it to vibrate at exactly the same rate.

Human beings have played musical instruments since long before the beginning of recorded history. Fragments of a bone flute were discovered in 1995 in Slovenia; carved between 43,000 and 82,000 years ago by a Neanderthal person, it is the oldest musical instrument ever found.

The harp, violin, and piano produce music through the vibration of strings. Musicians pluck the strings with their fingers, stroke them with the fine hairs on a bow, or cause felt-covered hammers to strike them. The sound of the vibrating strings is amplified as it reverberates through the frame of the instrument.

In some other instruments, the movement of air creates the musical sound. These instruments include brass instruments, such as the trombone, and woodwinds, such as the flute. Blowing into such an instrument causes a column of air to vibrate. There are different ways to produce this vibration. One can blow across the hole of the flute, blow past the reed of a clarinet, or vibrate the lips against the mouthpiece of a trombone. The pitch changes when the column of vibrating air is lengthened or shortened.

Many percussion instruments are drumlike; the musician strikes a material stretched over a hollow structure. The size of the interior space, the elasticity and thickness of the covering, and the object used to strike the instrument all affect the sound produced. Some percussion instruments— such as bells or cymbals—are solid and vibrate when struck by another object.

Musical instruments have been made from different metals, all kinds of wood, fabric, glass, bone, animal hide, and plastics. Alone or in groups, they can make an infinite array of sounds organized in innumerable patterns.

Reading Time _2:00_

Recalling Facts

1. Sound is
   - ❏ a. speed of the vibrating air.
   - ❏ b. a disturbance in the ear.
   - ❏ c. the vibration of air sensed by the ear.

2. Harmony is
   - ❏ a. the change in the speed of auditory vibrations.
   - ❏ b. the sound of two or more notes played at the same time.
   - ❏ c. a beautiful musical sound.

3. A _____ is the oldest known musical instrument.
   - ❏ a. bone flute
   - ❏ b. wooden drum
   - ❏ c. vibrating string

4. Which of the following instruments does *not* produce sound through something being struck?
   - ❏ a. piano
   - ❏ b. trombone
   - ❏ c. cymbals

5. The pitch of the sound in a wind instrument depends on the _____ of the column of vibrating air.
   - ❏ a. force
   - ❏ b. length
   - ❏ c. width

Understanding Ideas

6. From the context of the article, you can infer that the word *auditory* has to do with
   - ❏ a. feeling.
   - ❏ b. seeing.
   - ❏ c. hearing.

7. If two instruments are playing two different notes, you can assume that the instruments
   - ❏ a. are making the air vibrate at different rates.
   - ❏ b. are different types of instruments.
   - ❏ c. are not creating harmony.

8. Because hammers strike the strings of the piano to make sound, a piano
   - ❏ a. might be thought of as a wind instrument.
   - ❏ b. might also be considered a percussion instrument.
   - ❏ c. might be considered a form of a violin.

9. What would happen if recorded music were played in an airless room?
   - ❏ a. The sound would be very loud.
   - ❏ b. The music would be very slow.
   - ❏ c. There would be no sound.

10. Which of the following is *not* true?
    - ❏ a. Both violin and trombone players may pluck the strings of their instruments.
    - ❏ b. Trombone and flute players learn different ways to blow air into their instruments.
    - ❏ c. Many percussion instruments are drumlike.

Although different cultures have produced similar musical instruments—harps, drums, and flutes, for instance—the sound and structure of each culture's music is unique.

The music that developed on the European continent is organized around a scale of 12 tones arranged in sequence by pitch. The relationships between these notes are the same for classical symphonies, country ballads, and even heavy metal.

Principles of the raga, an important melodic form in India's Hindu music, were established by the second century. Ragas are constructed from a scale of 22 tones, each about equal to one-quarter of a whole tone of the European scale. The range of sounds possible, therefore, is wide. Ragas are often played on stringed instruments and accompanied by intricate drummed rhythms.

In the 1950s, Chinese scholars classified 1,500 years of their region's music, using four categories: folk songs, opera, narrative singing, and instrumental music. In Chinese music, the tone of the sound matters more than the notes of the melody. Chinese instruments are, therefore, classified by the materials from which they are made: gourd, bamboo, wood, silk, clay, metal, stone, and animal skin.

The music of the native peoples of sub-Saharan Africa is distinguished by its complex rhythms. Many African instruments are of the percussion type: xylophones, rattles, and a vast array of drums. African music also commonly employs the sounds of bamboo flutes and a one-stringed bow.

1. Recognizing Words in Context

Find the word *intricate* in the passage. One definition below is closest to the meaning of that word. One definition has the opposite or nearly opposite meaning. The remaining definition has a completely different meaning. Label the definitions C for *closest*, O for *opposite or nearly opposite*, and D for *different*.

_____ a. complex

_____ b. simple

_____ c. repetitious

2. Distinguishing Fact from Opinion

Two of the statements below present *facts*, which can be proved correct. The other statement is an *opinion*, which expresses someone's thoughts or beliefs. Label the statements F for *fact* and O for *opinion*.

_____ a. Most European music is based on a 12-tone scale.

_____ b. Chinese instruments are identified according to what they are made from.

_____ c. African music is fascinating to listen to.

3. Keeping Events in Order

Label the statements below 1, 2, and 3 to show the order in which the events happened

_____ a. Principles of the Hindu raga were set.

_____ b. Chinese put traditional music into four categories.

_____ c. The first Europeans who arrived in North America brought their music with them.

4. Making Correct Inferences

Two of the statements below are correct *inferences*, or reasonable guesses. They are based on information in the passage. The other statement is an incorrect, or faulty, inference. Label the statements C for *correct* inference and F for *faulty* inference.

_____ a. Instruments that are alike create different music in different cultures.

_____ b. Chinese music is more ancient than that of India and Africa.

_____ c. Music of different countries can often be identified without seeing the musicians.

5. Understanding Main Ideas

One of the statements below expresses the main idea of the passage. One statement is too general, or too broad. The other explains only part of the passage; it is too narrow. Label the statements M for *main idea*, B for *too broad*, and N for *too narrow*.

_____ a. Most cultures include harps, drums, and flutes in their musical forms.

_____ b. Different cultures have created unique musical systems out of similar sounds.

_____ c. There are many types of music.

Correct Answers, Part A ___9___

Correct Answers, Part B ___11___

Total Correct Answers ___20___

Technology and the History of Communications

Communications is a collective term for the many methods of sharing information. Written language allows people to communicate with one another across distances and through time because a written document communicates the same information to different people. Spoken information is often repeated from person to person, and the message may get distorted in the process.

The first innovation in what might be thought of as modern communications took place in the mid-1400s when Johannes Gutenberg printed a Bible on his movable-type printing press. As a result of Gutenberg's innovation, many copies of a text could be quickly distributed across large areas. The cost of information and the difficulty of acquiring it were greatly reduced. During the four centuries that followed this breakthrough, however, the only improvements in the technology were minor changes in the machines and materials. Moreover, the speed of communications remained equal to the speed of the person or vehicle delivering the message.

Beginning in 1837, messages in the form of electromagnetic impulses could be sent through wires using the code of "dits" and "dahs" devised by Samuel F. B. Morse. Then, in 1876, only decades after the birth of the telegraph, Alexander Graham Bell summoned his assistant from another room by saying "Watson, come here. I want you" into a machine. His telephone was introduced to the public just two months later. The next year Thomas Edison recorded the words "Mary had a little lamb" and invented the phonograph, on which the recording could be played.

By the end of the century, communications had become wireless. Guglielmo Marconi patented his "black box"—an early radio—in 1896. In the 1930s television technology added pictures to sound; by the 1950s, TV sets were common in American homes. In the 1960s, satellites orbiting Earth made it possible to transmit radio and TV signals around the world in an instant.

The next milestone in communications would prove to be a monumental one—the computer. An invention hastened by the needs of the military during World War II, the first computer was a huge machine. In 1971, the microprocessor chip ushered in the era of small computers. ARPANET, a network of government and university researchers, evolved into the Internet, now traveled by people of all ages and backgrounds. By the 21st century, what had once been a rugged road of communications had become a well-paved information superhighway.

Reading Time _1:50 sec_

Recalling Facts

1. The term *communications* refers
   - ❏ a. to all methods of sharing information.
   - ❏ b. only to conversations between people.
   - ❏ c. only to varieties of written languages.

2. Telegraph messages
   - ❏ a. are letters written in code.
   - ❏ b. were the first important innovation in communications.
   - ❏ c. are electromagnetic impulses sent over wires.

3. Bell invented the telephone in
   - ❏ a. 1896.
   - ❏ b. 1876.
   - ❏ c. 1776.

4. Radio was the first form of
   - ❏ a. long-distance communication using the human voice.
   - ❏ b. wireless communication.
   - ❏ c. long distance communication to depend on electricity.

5. Personal computers first became available
   - ❏ a. in the 21st century.
   - ❏ b. at the end of World War II.
   - ❏ c. after 1971.

Understanding Ideas

6. One could conclude from this article that communications technology
   - ❏ a. grew most quickly after the 19th century.
   - ❏ b. made its greatest advances before the 19th century.
   - ❏ c. evolved at a steady pace throughout history.

7. In ancient times, most people probably were not
   - ❏ a. interested in knowing about events in nearby areas.
   - ❏ b. well-informed about events outside of their own community.
   - ❏ c. able to understand the meaning of events going on in faraway places.

8. Technologies like the telegraph and the telephone
   - ❏ a. needed experienced operators in every neighborhood.
   - ❏ b. were not useful inventions at first.
   - ❏ c. depended on wires strung from one place to another.

9. You can infer that the telegraph was invented by
   - ❏ a. Samuel F. B. Morse.
   - ❏ b. Alexander Graham Bell.
   - ❏ c. Guglielmo Marconi.

10. One could conclude from this article that computers probably became more useful to ordinary people
    - ❏ a. once computer courses were taught in schools.
    - ❏ b. after the invention of the microprocessor chip.
    - ❏ c. once World War II was over.

Cryptography and Cryptology: Figure It Out

Since written language was created, people have devised ways to keep the contents of their spoken and written messages secret. Cryptography is the process of translating unfamiliar writing systems. Cryptographers have found the keys to unlock unusual written languages such as Egyptian hieroglyphics or Sumerian cuneiform. They can also focus on the making and breaking of codes. People who turn meaningful text into a meaningless series of symbols—and change ciphered text back into readable form—are called cryptologists.

To illustrate the value of cryptologists, consider the Native American "code talkers" of World War II. Frustrated by Japan's skill at cracking U.S. military codes, the U.S. Marine Corps found what they needed in the Navajo language. This language proved to be the perfect encryption system. It is very complex but has no written form, neither alphabet nor symbols. It was known only to a small number of people, most of whom lived in the southwestern United States. During the war, the code talkers never made a serious mistake in the information they transmitted, nor were their codes ever broken. Sworn to secrecy in this top-secret project in 1942, the 29 original code talkers received no official recognition for their work until 2001, when they were awarded the Congressional Gold Medal (25 of them posthumously, or after their deaths).

(1:05 sec)

1. **Recognizing Words in Context**

   Find the word *ciphered* in the passage. One definition below is closest to the meaning of that word. One definition has the opposite or nearly opposite meaning. The remaining definition has a completely different meaning. Label the definitions C for *closest,* O for *opposite or nearly opposite,* and D for *different.*

   _____ a. foreign

   _____ b. coded

   _____ c. decoded

2. **Distinguishing Fact from Opinion**

   Two of the statements below present *facts,* which can be proved correct. The other statement is an *opinion,* which expresses someone's thoughts or beliefs. Label the statements F for *fact* and O for *opinion.*

   _____ a. The Japanese cracked U.S. military codes at the outset of World War II.

   _____ b. People who use codes for everyday messages are ridiculous.

   _____ c. The Navajo code talkers never made a serious mistake.

3. Keeping Events in Order

Label the statements below 1, 2, and 3 to show the order in which the events happened.

_____ a. Navajo code talkers began transmitting messages for the U.S. military.

_____ b. The Japanese successfully interpreted many U.S. military communications.

_____ c. Many fewer military messages were deciphered by the Japanese.

4. Making Correct Inferences

Two of the statements below are correct *inferences*, or reasonable guesses. They are based on information in the passage. The other statement is an incorrect, or faulty, inference. Label the statements C for *correct* inference and F for *faulty* inference.

_____ a. The Navajo language is not difficult to learn.

_____ b. Cryptology is almost as old as written language.

_____ c. The military often makes use of cryptographers.

5. Understanding Main Ideas

One of the statements below expresses the main idea of the passage. One statement is too general, or too broad. The other explains only part of the passage; it is too narrow. Label the statements M for *main idea*, B for *too broad*, and N for *too narrow*.

_____ a. People have different ways of communicating secretly.

_____ b. Japanese cryptologists were unable to crack the Navajo code.

_____ c. Cryptography is the study of unfamiliar languages and codes.

Correct Answers, Part A _10____

Correct Answers, Part B _____

Total Correct Answers _____

Transparency: Seeing Through It

A material can be transparent, opaque, or translucent. These three words describe the extent to which a given material allows radiant energy— electromagnetic radiation in particular—to pass through it. Radiant energy in the form of visible light includes electromagnetic radiation of a variety of wavelengths. The human eye perceives these wavelengths as colors. A beam of white or colorless light such as sunlight includes all the hues of the spectrum: red, orange, yellow, green, blue, and violet.

A transparent medium—such as glass—neither reflects light nor refracts it as it passes through, and it absorbs little energy in the form of heat. When a beam of light is refracted, it bends. The extent to which a substance is transparent is determined by the total amount of electromagnetic radiation that passes through it. The less light that is reflected, refracted, or absorbed, the more transparent the material.

An opaque medium—such as stone, metal, or wood—appears solid and is impervious to light rays of particular wavelengths. An opaque medium both blocks and absorbs electromagnetic radiation and will appear to be the color of the particular wavelengths it reflects. A board painted green, for instance, reflects both yellow and blue wavelengths and absorbs the rest. It does not, however, transmit any light.

A translucent medium is neither transparent nor opaque but somewhere in between, diffusing the light it allows through. Objects seen through a translucent medium may look shadowy, blurred, or distorted. Some materials are translucent only when they are in a thin layer. These include some kinds of porcelain and plastic. Glass that is transparent in thin layers may be translucent in thick layers.

A material's transparency is a measure of the total amount of light in the beam that is transmitted through the material. Energy that is absorbed or reflected by a substance decreases the amount of energy transmitted and so lessens the degree to which that substance is transparent. Nothing is perfectly transparent and can transmit 100 percent of light's energy. Glass, however, is classified loosely as a transparent material. A number of glasses are "selectively transparent," meaning that they transmit light of one wavelength or color more efficiently than any other. The red light of a traffic light is actually a red lens in front of a clear white light bulb. The lens transmits red light and absorbs all other colors; all the eye can perceive is red light.

Reading Time _2 min_

Recalling Facts

1. Another name for light is
   - ❏ a. electromagnetic radiation.
   - ❏ b. wavelength.
   - ❏ c. spectrum.

2. A transparent material
   - ❏ a. refracts light.
   - ❏ b. lets electromagnetic radiation pass through.
   - ❏ c. absorbs a lot of radiant energy as heat.

3. Which of the following is *not* true of an opaque medium?
   - ❏ a. It appears solid.
   - ❏ b. It is impervious to most light rays.
   - ❏ c. It does not reflect light.

4. When placed behind a translucent medium, objects
   - ❏ a. are fully visible.
   - ❏ b. are invisible.
   - ❏ c. may appear blurry.

5. Which of the following statements is true?
   - ❏ a. A perfectly transparent material would transmit all electromagnetic radiation.
   - ❏ b. Glass is a perfectly transparent material.
   - ❏ c. A selectively transparent material absorbs most light as heat.

Understanding Ideas

6. One can conclude from this passage that
   - ❏ a. light and color are separate forms of energy.
   - ❏ b. heat is not a form of energy.
   - ❏ c. visible light is not the only type of electromagnetic radiation.

7. If you are wearing a violet-colored shirt, then you may conclude that the fabric
   - ❏ a. reflects all light wavelengths except violet.
   - ❏ b. absorbs all wavelengths except violet.
   - ❏ c. is transparent.

8. Which of the following inferences is correct?
   - ❏ a. All types of stone are translucent when cut very thin.
   - ❏ b. No type of stone can ever be made translucent.
   - ❏ c. Thin layers of some types of stone are translucent.

9. A material that lets through a small amount of visible light may be described as
   - ❏ a. opaque.
   - ❏ b. translucent.
   - ❏ c. transparent.

10. If 90 percent of light is absorbed by a material and 10 percent is reflected by it, the material
    - ❏ a. must be opaque.
    - ❏ b. is probably opaque.
    - ❏ c. cannot be opaque.

Glass, that lovely and apparently fragile material, is a noncrystalline substance formed by the fusion of silicate material with soda and lime under very high temperatures. Usually translucent or transparent, glass can be imbued with a rainbow of colors. Sunlight streaming through stained-glass windows casts a mosaic of jewel-like hues on the walls and floors beyond.

The color in glass comes from particles suspended in the mixture. One common way to color glass is to add a metallic oxide. People make metallic oxides by dissolving metals in acid. Different oxides produce different colors: uranium oxide produces a vivid yellow-green color, and gold chloride turns glass a rich ruby red. The presence of iron in glass can produce shades of green, amber, or brown; copper makes glass a light blue; cobalt gives it a very dark blue tint; manganese results in shades of purple; and lead antimony yields yellow.

The stained-glass compositional technique of fastening pieces of colored glass together with lead strips, copper, or cement dates at least as far back as the Roman Empire. Decorative stained-glass windows were first used in churches; some of these windows, such as those in southern Germany's Augsburg Cathedral, have been in place for more than 1,000 years.

(1 min)

1. **Recognizing Words in Context**

   Find the word *fusion* in the passage. One definition below is closest to the meaning of that word. One definition has the opposite or nearly opposite meaning. The remaining definition has a completely different meaning. Label the definitions C for *closest,* O for *opposite or nearly opposite,* and D for *different.*

   _____ a. invention

   _____ b. separation

   _____ c. combination

2. **Distinguishing Fact from Opinion**

   Two of the statements below present *facts,* which can be proved correct. The other statement is an *opinion,* which expresses someone's thoughts or beliefs. Label the statements F for *fact* and O for *opinion.*

   _____ a. Uranium oxide turns glass yellow green.

   _____ b. Stained glass is gorgeous and delicate.

   _____ c. Ancient Romans made stained-glass windows.

3. Keeping Events in Order

Label the statements below 1, 2, and 3 to show the order in which the events happen.

_____ a. Silica and other ingredients are melted over high heat.

_____ b. An artist uses lead strips to connect pieces of colored glass.

_____ c. A metallic oxide is added to color the glass mixture.

4. Making Correct Inferences

Two of the statements below are correct *inferences,* or reasonable guesses. They are based on information in the passage. The other statement is an incorrect, or faulty, inference. Label the statements C for *correct* inference and F for *faulty* inference.

_____ a. The craft of glassmaking is ancient.

_____ b. There are various ways to imbue glass with color.

_____ c. All colored glass contains metal oxide.

5. Understanding Main Ideas

One of the statements below expresses the main idea of the passage. One statement is too general, or too broad. The other explains only part of the passage; it is too narrow. Label the statements M for *main idea*, B for *too broad,* and N for *too narrow.*

_____ a. The process of making stained glass consists of several steps.

_____ b. Glassmaking has a long history.

_____ c. Color in glass results from particles suspended in the glass.

Correct Answers, Part A ___9___

Correct Answers, Part B _____

Total Correct Answers _____

12　A　Fall Foliage

The blazing colors of fall foliage create a remarkable contrast with the full green of summer and the bare branches of winter. Fall colors seem to appear within a matter of days, only to disappear after a few good strong breezes. These colors are largely the result of a slowing in photosynthesis. Photosynthesis is the process through which light energy from the sun, water absorbed through a plant's roots, and carbon dioxide from the air are converted to carbohydrates and oxygen in the presence of chlorophyll.

Photosynthesis takes place primarily in a plant's leaves. It creates the glucose and other carbohydrates that support growth and that can be stored for use during the winter. Also during photosynthesis, leaves release oxygen back into the atmosphere. Chlorophyll is the chemical that enables the process of photosynthesis, and its large molecules contain a green pigment that colors the leaves. Chlorophyll is fragile, however—bright sunlight causes chlorophyll to decompose, and it must be constantly regenerated during the warm months of summer.

The steady decrease in sunlight following the summer solstice gradually slows photosynthesis, and eventually cooler temperatures impede the regeneration of chlorophyll. Diminutive tubes at the base of each leaf carry water into the leaf and food back to the tree through abscission cells. In the fall, the cells of the abscission layer begin to swell; they reduce and finally cut off the exchange of fluids, trapping glucose and waste products in the leaves. Without the warmth of the summer sun or a constant supply of fresh water, the chlorophyll disintegrates and disappears.

Divested of its green suit of chlorophyll, a leaf finally displays its true colors. The foliage of birches, tulip poplars, and hickory trees becomes butter yellow and gold, confirming the presence of the pigments xanthophyll and carotene. Reds and purples signal elevated levels of glucose residues in the leaves. Anthocyanin, found in red maple, red oak, and sumac leaves, interacts with sugars, proteins, and acids to create a broad range of reds—crimson, burgundy, and fuchsia. Some leaves contain a variety of pigments that combine to make such intermediate colors as orange. The waste product tannin turns leaves brown. These substances, along with the last green traces of chlorophyll, paint individual leaves, as well as the view at large, in gorgeous and variegated color. When sunny days alternate with cool nights after a dry end to the summer, fall colors are especially striking.

Reading Time _2 min_

Recalling Facts

1. Green color indicates the presence of _____ in leaves.
   - ❏ a. chlorophyll
   - ❏ b. xanthophyll
   - ❏ c. glucose

2. Photosynthesis requires the presence of
   - ❏ a. water, oxygen, and light.
   - ❏ b. water, carbon dioxide, and light.
   - ❏ c. water, chlorophyll, and oxygen.

3. Abscission cells control
   - ❏ a. the exchange of fluids between the leaf and the tree.
   - ❏ b. the amount of glucose the leaf manufactures.
   - ❏ c. the tree's storage of carbohydrates.

4. Both _____ and _____ contain anthocyanin.
   - ❏ a. birches; red maples
   - ❏ b. hickory trees; beets
   - ❏ c. sumac; red oaks

5. Fall foliage is most colorful when
   - ❏ a. there was plentiful rain in August.
   - ❏ b. sunny days alternate with cool nights.
   - ❏ c. the summer was long and hot.

Understanding Ideas

6. Which of the following is an appropriate inference?
   - ❏ a. The healthiest trees have the brightest fall colors.
   - ❏ b. Without chlorophyll, a tree will die within days.
   - ❏ c. Photosynthesis replenishes the air with oxygen.

7. One could conclude from this article that if the beginning of autumn were unusually warm,
   - ❏ a. chlorophyll would rapidly disappear from leaves.
   - ❏ b. leaves would change color later than usual.
   - ❏ c. trees would have trouble storing enough food for the winter.

8. A long drought starting in the middle of the summer would likely result in
   - ❏ a. a significant increase in the amount of chlorophyll in leaves.
   - ❏ b. trees' using up most of their stored glucose.
   - ❏ c. leaves' changing color earlier than usual.

9. One could conclude from this article that birch and tulip poplar leaves contain little or no
   - ❏ a. carotene.
   - ❏ b. chlorophyll.
   - ❏ c. anthocyanin.

10. One could infer that green foliage
    - ❏ a. indicates photosynthetic activity.
    - ❏ b. always turns red or yellow in the autumn.
    - ❏ c. contributes significant amounts of carbon dioxide to the atmosphere.

Around September 23 each year, the Sun appears to move southward to the equator, where it is equidistant from Earth's poles. At this time, there are 12 hours of daylight and 12 hours of darkness.

This is the autumnal equinox, which marks the apogee of the harvest season in the Northern Hemisphere, and the full moon that occurs just after it is called the harvest moon. The harvest moon rises close to sunset, brilliantly illuminating the landscape and allowing farmers, particularly those in the northern latitudes, to work late into the night.

As it lifts above the horizon, the harvest moon often has a brilliant gold color; this, however, is only an illusion. The light that seems to emanate from the harvest moon is actually reflected by Earth. As the light passes through Earth's atmosphere, mostly blue light waves are filtered out, allowing the yellow end of the spectrum to dominate.

Throughout history—and around the globe—the autumnal equinox has been a time of both celebration and preparation. People of different cultural backgrounds give thanks for summer's fruitfulness while anticipating the hardships that the upcoming winter months may bring. In Japan, the day of the autumnal equinox is a national holiday, the high point of a weeklong celebration during which people also pay their respects to the dead. In Korea, the event is celebrated by the making of moon cakes, the traditional food of harvest and thanksgiving.

(1:15)

1. **Recognizing Words in Context**

Find the word *apogee* in the passage. One definition below is closest to the meaning of that word. One definition has the opposite or nearly opposite meaning. The remaining definition has a completely different meaning. Label the definitions C for *closest*, O for *opposite or nearly opposite*, and D for *different*.

_____ a. length

_____ b. peak

_____ c. low point

2. **Distinguishing Fact from Opinion**

Two of the statements below present *facts*, which can be proved correct. The other statement is an *opinion*, which expresses someone's thoughts or beliefs. Label the statements F for *fact* and O for *opinion*.

_____ a. The Sun is an equal distance from the North and South Poles at the equinox.

_____ b. The light of the harvest moon is beautiful.

_____ c. The equinox traditionally is a time of celebration.

3. Keeping Events in Order

Label the statements below 1, 2, and 3 to show the order in which the events happen.

_____ a. Day and night are equal in length.

_____ b. The harvest moon rises over the horizon.

_____ c. The Sun appears to move south out of the northern sky.

4. Making Correct Inferences

Two of the statements below are correct *inferences,* or reasonable guesses. They are based on information in the passage. The other statement is an incorrect, or faulty, inference. Label the statements C for *correct* inference and F for *faulty* inference.

_____ a. Winter represents a time of hardship.

_____ b. Autumn is the traditional harvest season around the world.

_____ c. Following the autumnal equinox, nights are longer than days.

5. Understanding Main Ideas

One of the statements below expresses the main idea of the passage. One statement is too general, or too broad. The other explains only part of the passage; it is too narrow. Label the statements M for *main idea,* B for *too broad, and* N for *too narrow.*

_____ a. The harvest moon rises near the time of the autumnal equinox.

_____ b. The autumn equinox, when day and night are equal in length, occurs in the harvest season of the Northern Hemisphere.

_____ c. The amount of daylight varies according to the time of the year.

Correct Answers, Part A _____9_____

Correct Answers, Part B _____9_____

Total Correct Answers _____18_____

Barnacles are familiar as the sharp-shelled creatures that attach themselves to the sides of ships. Scuba divers and swimmers know them as a source of cut feet and scraped hands. But barnacles are also a traditional food for Native American tribes living in the Pacific Northwest. Originally thought to be related to such mollusks as clams and oysters, barnacles actually constitute the subclass Cirripedia of the class Crustacea, a class that also includes lobsters and crabs.

The barnacles that people see most often are acorn barnacles, found in temperate and cold oceans, and stalked barnacles, usually found in warmer seas. These creatures cement themselves to wooden piers, boats, rocks, and the smooth skin of whales and large fish. To do this they use an adhesive substance produced by a gland located on their antennae. Barnacles also secrete calcium carbonate to form their shells, which are called carapaces. Carapaces are commonly white but also can be yellow, orange, or pink. The animal itself can range in length from under 1 to 75 centimeters (0.5 to 30 inches) and feeds primarily on tiny organic particles and plankton. Their feathery, jointed legs, called cirri, extend from the shell and sweep food toward the mouth located deep inside the shell. Barnacles absorb oxygen from the water through their cirri and also through their body wall. They are able to close their shells tightly and maintain a watery environment within that helps them survive in the open air during low tides.

Most barnacles are hermaphrodites, possessing both male and female organs, but a barnacle typically fertilizes another barnacle's eggs and not its own. Fertilized eggs are carried in the mantle cavity, the space between the shell and the body tissue. When the eggs hatch into free-swimming larvae called nauplius larvae, the parent barnacle releases the larvae into the water. After the nauplius larva molts, it becomes a cypris larva and ceases to eat. The cypris larva can survive in the open water up to 13 days, during which time it must find some surface on which it can live out its life, a period usually lasting three to five years. The cypris larva uses its first pair of antenna to find a surface to which it can attach itself. Within 12 hours, it produces the plates that form its shell. When the shell is completed, the barnacle is considered to be an adult. Barnacles often cluster together to form colonies.

Reading Time _____

Recalling Facts

1. Barnacles are most closely related to
   - ❑ a. whales.
   - ❑ b. oysters.
   - ❑ c. crabs.

2. Which of the following is *not* true of a barnacle's shell?
   - ❑ a. It can be moved to a new location.
   - ❑ b. It is made of calcium carbonate secreted by the barnacle.
   - ❑ c. It can be sealed off against the air.

3. After the fertilized eggs hatch, the larvae first
   - ❑ a. begin to secrete shells.
   - ❑ b. attach themselves to a surface and begin to feed.
   - ❑ c. are released into the water.

4. Cypris larvae
   - ❑ a. hatch from the fertilized eggs of the barnacle.
   - ❑ b. can survive up to 13 days without food.
   - ❑ c. collect food with their legs.

5. Which of the following statements is *not* true?
   - ❑ a. It takes a few days for a barnacle to build its shell.
   - ❑ b. Acorn barnacles live in temperate and cold waters.
   - ❑ c. Barnacles feed on plankton.

Understanding Ideas

6. One could conclude from this article that barnacles
   - ❑ a. harm the whales to which they attach themselves.
   - ❑ b. are good to eat.
   - ❑ c. are found in fresh water.

7. Which of the following words best describes most barnacles?
   - ❑ a. migratory
   - ❑ b. sedentary
   - ❑ c. mobile

8. Barnacles belong to the subclass Cirripedia. If *cirri* comes from a Latin word meaning "curl," then *pedia* most likely means
   - ❑ a. head.
   - ❑ b. body.
   - ❑ c. foot.

9. A nauplius larva
   - ❑ a. depends on the parent barnacle for food.
   - ❑ b. finds a surface to which to attach itself.
   - ❑ c. eats plankton and tiny organic particles.

10. Why might some species of barnacles have spread to coastal areas around the world?
    - ❑ a. They have been taken to different locations by whales and boats.
    - ❑ b. The larvae are excellent long-distance swimmers.
    - ❑ c. The species evolved in many different areas at approximately the same time.

Watch Out for Some Marine Life

In addition to sharks, many other aggressive animals, including barracudas, eels, and jellyfish, thrive in the oceans—as do a number of other creatures that are able to inflict painful wounds. It is wise for people to be cautious in the marine environment.

Barracudas, with their needle-like teeth, have an unfair reputation for hostility. Barracudas are unlikely to attack humans, but they are territorial and can be a problem for people who are spearfishing. The spotted moray eel is nocturnal and lives in quiet places such as holes in the ocean floor and sunken wrecks. Its menacing appearance is due to the razor-sharp teeth exposed as it breathes. It can pose a risk to divers.

A number of marine animals, such as jellyfish, possess stingers called nematocysts. Jellyfish look like shiny iridescent bubbles trailing transparent ribbons, but they are dangerous both alive and dead: nematocysts located in their tentacles can sting even when removed from the jellyfish. One of the most poisonous jellyfish is the violet-pink Portuguese man-of-war.

Some sponges, including the reddish-orange fire sponge and the poison-bun sponge, can produce contact dermatitis, which causes redness of the skin and swelling. Sea urchins are soft-bodied creatures inside an armor of sharp spines; in many species, these spines are poisonous. In addition to the discomfort caused by the puncture and the toxin, infection can set in if the spine is not completely removed from the wound.

(1:15)

1. **Recognizing Words in Context**

   Find the word *iridescent* in the passage. One definition is closets in meaning to that world. One definition has the opposite or nearly opposite meaning. The remaining definition has a completely different meaning. Label the definitions C for *closest*, O for *opposite or nearly opposite*, and D for *different*.

   _____ a. glistening

   _____ b. saturated

   _____ c. dull

2. **Distinguishing Fact from Opinion**

   Two of the statements below present *facts*, which can be proved correct. The other statement is an *opinion*, which expresses someone's thoughts or beliefs. Label the statements F for *fact* and O for *opinion*.

   _____ a. Jellyfish look like iridescent bubbles.

   _____ b. Barracudas rarely attack people.

   _____ c. Sea urchins are protected by an armor of sharp spines.

3. Keeping Events in Order

Label the statements below 1, 2, and 3 to show the order in which the events happen.

_____ a. Barracudas appear ready to attack a swimmer.

_____ b. A swimmer begins to spear small fish.

_____ c. A swimmer enters the water and notices many species of fish, including barracudas.

4. Making Correct Inferences

Two of the statements below are correct *inferences*, or reasonable guesses. They are based on information in the passage. The other statement is an incorrect, or faulty, inference. Label the statements C for *correct* inference and F for *faulty* inference.

_____ a. Many marine animals have evolved defenses that are toxic to other creatures.

_____ b. Most people who swim in the ocean are wounded by an animal sooner or later.

_____ c. Jellyfish stings are a common type of injury inflicted by marine creatures.

5. Understanding Main Ideas

One of the statements below expresses the main idea of the passage. One statement is too general, or too broad. The other explains only part of the passage; it is too narrow. Label the statements M for *main idea*, B for *too broad*, and N for *too narrow*.

_____ a. The ocean is the habitat of a wide range of fish, mammals, and invertebrates.

_____ b. There are dangerous life forms in the oceans.

_____ c. Divers and spearfishers may encounter dangerous life forms in the oceans.

Correct Answers, Part A ___8___

Correct Answers, Part B ___15___

Total Correct Answers ___23___

Archaeologists search for clues that help form a clearer picture of the lives people led in the past. Archaeology is a modern science, but it has been evolving for centuries. More than 2,400 years ago, the Greek historian Herodotus described the Egyptian pyramids and other monuments. He may have been the first writer to consider that relics and ruins could provide information for later generations. For more than a millennium, however, such scholars were observers rather than researchers.

In the 1700s, scientists and adventurers from a variety of countries traveled far and wide to explore ancient sites. Excavations that are still in progress began in 1709 at Herculaneum, an Italian city buried in ash during the eruption of Mount Vesuvius in A.D. 79. The Danish scholar Carsten Niebuhr visited the ruins of Persepolis in the Middle East in 1765 to study cuneiform writing. It was not until the 19th century, however, that archaeology became a widely recognized science and schools recognized the subject as a scholarly pursuit. The term itself was coined in 1837. It comes from a Latin word meaning "the study of antiquities." One of the first archaeologists to use a scientific approach to the discipline was Heinrich Schliemann of Germany, who in the late 1800s investigated the ancient civilization of Troy.

Today, archaeologists uncover the past in many different locations, including deserts and jungles, at sites called digs. Ancient sources, folklore, and landscape features can suggest where archaeologists should look. Surveys of the land help them choose sites likely to yield artifacts, the objects that will unlock the story of a particular people—their daily lives, their beliefs, and their ties to other cultures. However, a site does not have to be old to be interesting to an archaeologist. Some prefer to study more recent settlements. One scientist, for instance, studies coal mining camps in California by examining the garbage that miners left behind.

Archaeologists use skills and knowledge from many subjects, including geology, biology, chemistry, statistics, the social sciences, and art. Archaeologists may work for universities, museums, governments, or private firms. Some are involved in educating the public about protecting ancient sites. Artifact hunters ignorant of history ransack these places and sell what they find for a few dollars to unscrupulous dealers in antiquities. A variety of public works projects—such as dams, roads, and building construction—also threaten digs and other historical sites.

Reading Time _____

Recalling Facts

1. Archaeology is the study of
   - ❑ a. architecture.
   - ❑ b. ancient artifacts.
   - ❑ c. soil conservation.

2. Archaeological methods became scientific
   - ❑ a. in the 19th century.
   - ❑ b. in the 18th century.
   - ❑ c. in A.D. 79.

3. Which archaeologist studied the ancient civilization of Troy?
   - ❑ a. Carsten Niebuhr
   - ❑ b. Heinrich Schliemann
   - ❑ c. Herodotus

4. Which of the following statements is *not* true?
   - ❑ a. Archaeologists may work in deserts.
   - ❑ b. A dig may need specialists in art, geology, and botany.
   - ❑ c. People respect important artifacts enough not to steal them.

5. Which of the following does *not* pose a danger to archaeological sites?
   - ❑ a. public works projects
   - ❑ b. unscrupulous dealers in antiquities
   - ❑ c. a survey of the physical features of a region

Understanding Ideas

6. One could conclude that archaeologists
   - ❑ a. need a broad education.
   - ❑ b. are primarily concerned with finding precious objects.
   - ❑ c. rarely have college degrees.

7. Which of the following *cannot* be inferred from this article?
   - ❑ a. People have always been curious about past civilizations.
   - ❑ b. Objects people throw away can be as important to study as objects they preserve.
   - ❑ c. Archaeologists are most interested in gold and jewels.

8. The fact that excavations at Herculaneum are still in progress most likely suggests that
   - ❑ a. archaeologists work slowly to stay employed for decades.
   - ❑ b. the city was large and was buried completely.
   - ❑ c. at times, archaeologists have lost interest in the excavations.

9. Someone studying to be an archaeologist would have the least use for knowledge in the subject of
   - ❑ a. physics.
   - ❑ b. sociology.
   - ❑ c. history.

10. If a Greek vase made in 600 B.C. was found at a dig in Egypt, one might conclude that
    - ❑ a. Greece and Egypt were part of the same country.
    - ❑ b. Greece and Egypt sometimes traded goods with each other.
    - ❑ c. Greek vases are worthless.

The earth is composed of layers, or strata, that usually correspond to historical or geological periods. This fact provides archaeologists with a known framework that they use to organize artifacts found during the course of a dig.

Before they dig, archaeologists first must create an accurate map of the site; they then dig shallow, square holes called units. Trowels, dental tools, toothpicks, and even tiny brushes can be used to unearth artifacts, depending on the composition of the soil. The dirt removed is placed in buckets for later examination. Archaeologists use large tools such as shovels and backhoes very cautiously, and only when they are confident that such implements will not damage relic-rich deposits. As the archaeologists excavate, they keep a sharp eye out for any artifact, no matter how small. They take the dirt they save and sift it through screens in a search for such items as bits of stone tools, bone fragments, and pottery shards.

The data archaeologists collect are as important as the artifacts themselves, and every feature of the dig is carefully documented. Each stratum of earth is rigorously measured, analyzed, and described; relationships between various finds are evaluated and recorded. Artists and photographers provide a pictorial record of each item found and every facet of the procedure.

1. **Recognizing Words in Context**

   Find the word *rigorously* in the passage. One definition below is closest to the meaning of that word. One definition has the opposite or nearly opposite meaning. The remaining definition has a completely different meaning. Label the definitions C for *closest*, O for *opposite or nearly opposite*, and D for *different*.

   _____ a. inexactly

   _____ b. precisely

   _____ c. slightly

2. **Distinguishing Fact from Opinion**

   Two of the statements below present *facts*, which can be proved correct. The other statement is an *opinion*, which expresses someone's thoughts or beliefs. Label the statements F for *fact* and O for *opinion*.

   _____ a. The earth is made up of strata that correspond to geological periods.

   _____ b. Large shovels may destroy artifacts.

   _____ c. Archaeologists are some of the most careful people you will ever meet.

3. Keeping Events in Order

Label the statements below 1, 2, and 3 to show the order in which the events happen.

_____ a. Surveyors map the area.

_____ b. Buckets of dirt are sifted to search for fragments.

_____ c. Archaeologists dig units in carefully selected places.

4. Making Correct Inferences

Two of the statements below are correct *inferences,* or reasonable guesses. They are based on information in the passage. The other statement is an incorrect, or faulty, inference. Label the statements C for *correct* inference and F for *faulty* inference.

_____ a. There are likely to be many people at work on a dig.

_____ b. Careless digging destroys evidence that might provide information about artifacts.

_____ c. Larger artifacts are more important than smaller ones.

5. Understanding Main Ideas

One of the statements below expresses the main idea of the passage. One statement is too general, or too broad. The other explains only part of the passage; it is too narrow. Label the statements M for *main idea,* B for *too broad,* and N for *too narrow.*

_____ a. Digging for artifacts is a time-consuming and painstaking process.

_____ b. Archaeologists search for artifacts from different periods in different strata of the earth.

_____ c. Archaeologists can work either indoors or outside.

Correct Answers, Part A _____

Correct Answers, Part B _____

Total Correct Answers _____

15　A　Hippocrates and the Symptoms of Disease

The Greek physician Hippocrates, who lived during the fifth and fourth centuries B.C., is widely recognized as the father of medicine. He and his students separated the practice of medicine from superstition and ritual and made it a science based on objective observation and deductive reasoning. Historians credit Hippocrates with laying the foundation for the rules that still govern the way doctors should behave toward their patients. His great legacy to medical science, however, is more than the records he left cataloging symptoms and categorizing diseases. He viewed illness in the context of a person's overall health and behavior.

Symptoms are any changes—such as pain, fever, fatigue, or nausea—from a state regarded as normal. Hippocrates may have been the first to describe the symptoms of influenza as coughing, aches, and pain lasting about three days, along with fever and sweating. In 410 B.C. he recorded an outbreak of mumps on the island of Thasos. Afflicted people suffered from mild fever, swollen areas near the ears, often on both sides of the head, hoarseness, and dry coughs. He noticed that the disease attacked both children and adults. Men who went to exercise in the palestra and the gymnasium, however, became sick more often than women. He also mentioned that the disease was most severe in men.

Many of Hippocrates' observations are in a book of recommendations called the *Aphorisms*. He considered the nature of sleep, for instance, finding that it had both good and bad implications for health: "In whatever disease sleep is laborious, it is a deadly symptom; but if sleep does good, it is not deadly." He also counseled against too much or too little sleep: "Both sleep and insomnia, when immoderate, are bad."

Hippocrates distinguished between the illnesses of adults and children. He noted, for instance, that newborns and small children were prone to vomiting, coughs, sleeplessness, "inflammation of the navel," and ear infections. The elderly, on the other hand, suffered often from shortness of breath and other respiratory ailments including coughs. Other illnesses affecting the aged include arthritis, urinary tract problems, weakening vision, and "dullness of hearing."

Hippocrates' analysis of the role of diet and the environment in diseases appear in the book *Airs, Waters, and Places*. Others before him had described the symptoms of malaria, which we now know is carried by mosquitoes. Hippocrates, however, was the first to connect malaria outbreaks with the presence of stagnant water.

Reading Time _1:45_

Recalling Facts

1. Hippocrates thought medical treatments should
   - a. be based on objective observation.
   - b. include religious rituals.
   - c. come from traditional practices.

2. Symptoms of disease
   - a. occur when a person is normal.
   - b. are always different in each person.
   - c. include pain, fever, nausea, and other conditions that are not normal.

3. Hippocrates found that ear infections and vomiting were
   - a. common problems in the elderly.
   - b. common problems in infants.
   - c. common symptoms of the mumps.

4. Between which of the following did Hippocrates find a connection?
   - a. spiders and malaria
   - b. malaria and stagnant water
   - c. stagnant water and nausea

5. Hippocrates noticed that the mumps
   - a. struck only men and children.
   - b. was usually fatal.
   - c. was most severe in men.

Understanding Ideas

6. One could conclude from this article that Hippocrates
   - a. influenced the development of the medical profession.
   - b. wrote about the ideas of his teachers.
   - c. played a key role in the invention of surgical equipment.

7. You can infer that one of the key underlying concepts of Hippocrates' recommendations for avoiding disease was
   - a. exercise.
   - b. moderation.
   - c. positive thinking.

8. According to the information in the passage, which inference about Hippocrates is probably false?
   - a. He encouraged people to eat a healthy diet.
   - b. He believed that some environments caused bad health.
   - c. He believed that the diseases had equal effects on people of different ages.

9. On Thasos, it is likely that
   - a. most of the people at the palestra were women.
   - b. men spent more time with their children than women did.
   - c. women were healthier than men.

10. If Hippocrates were alive today, which of the following would probably surprise him the least?
    - a. open-heart surgery
    - b. older people's difficulty in hearing and seeing
    - c. the use of anesthesia

The Controversy over Herbal Medicines

Herbal remedies have existed for thousands of years. Even so, not all approaches to the use of herbs to treat disease are the same.

In the United States, herbs are sold, like vitamins, as dietary aids. Sometimes recommended by folk healers and homeopaths, herbal treatments are often used in addition to, or instead of, conventional medical care. Doctors are rarely trained in the use of herbs and may resist including them in the course of a treatment for a number of reasons. They cite the absence of standardized dosages, lack of quality control in the preparation of herbal medicines, and the dearth of clinical research proving the safety and benefits of traditional herbal remedies.

In China, herbs are often a part of standard health and medical practices. Although at ease with modern technology and pharmaceuticals, many Chinese doctors approach disease from a holistic point of view. Traditional Chinese medicine stresses the connection between mental and physical well-being. It also asserts that people should live in harmony with both their social environment and the natural world. Chinese herbal medicine seeks to correct imbalances within the patient's body, or between the patient and his or her environment. Chinese doctors trained in Western medicine still take advantage of herbal treatments and often write prescriptions that are filled not at the pharmacy but at the herbalist's shop.

(1 min)

1. **Recognizing Words in Context**

   Find the word *dearth* in the passage. One definition below is closest to the meaning of that word. One definition has the opposite or nearly opposite meaning. The remaining definition has a completely different meaning. Label the definitions C for *closest*, O for *opposite or nearly opposite*, and D for *different*.

   _____ a. lack

   _____ b. benefit

   _____ c. abundance

2. **Distinguishing Fact from Opinion**

   Two of the statements below present *facts*, which can be proved correct. The other statement is an *opinion*, which expresses someone's thoughts or beliefs. Label the statements F for *fact* and O for *opinion*.

   _____ a. People have used herbs to treat disease for thousands of years.

   _____ b. Herbs are often the best way to treat the symptoms of disease.

   _____ c. Modern Chinese medicine often combines traditional and modern practices.

3. Keeping Events in Order

Label the statements below 1, 2, and 3 to show the order in which the events happen.

_____ a. A patient hears positive reports about the effectiveness of an herbal remedy.

_____ b. The doctor advises against using the herb due to a lack of scientific research about its side effects.

_____ c. The patient consults with a doctor about the herb.

4. Making Correct Inferences

Two of the statements below are correct *inferences,* or reasonable guesses. They are based on information in the passage. The other statement is an incorrect, or faulty, inference. Label the statements C for *correct* inference and F for *faulty* inference.

_____ a. Most homeopaths have more experience with herbs and folk remedies than medical doctors do.

_____ b. Herbal remedies and modern drugs have the same rate of success.

_____ c. Chinese and American doctors often study the same subjects in medical school.

5. Understanding Main Ideas

One of the statements below expresses the main idea of the passage. One statement is too general, or too broad. The other explains only part of the passage; it is too narrow. Label the statements M for *main idea,* B for *too broad,* and N for *too narrow.*

_____ a. Chinese doctors often include herbal remedies in their medical treatments.

_____ b. People around the world have used herbs to treat disease for thousands of years.

_____ c. Doctors in China and doctors in the West view herbal remedies differently.

Correct Answers, Part A ___10___

Correct Answers, Part B ___15___

Total Correct Answers ___25___

16   A   The Respiratory System

Respiration is the act of breathing. It consists of two steps: inhaling oxygen, also called inspiration, and exhaling carbon dioxide, also called expiration. The mechanism that keeps us breathing is called the respiratory system. It consists of the upper and lower respiratory tracts and has two main functions: ventilation and gas exchange.

The upper respiratory tract is the part of the body where inspiration and expiration take place. This is the area dedicated to ventilation, and it is designed for the efficient intake and expulsion of large amounts of air. It includes the nose and nasal cavity, the sinus spaces behind the face, the larynx or voice box, and the trachea or windpipe. The cells lining the nasal cavity are called the ethmoidal air cells as they are located in the area of the ethmoid bone, a light, spongy bone through which the olfactory nerves conduct sensations of smell to the brain.

The lower respiratory tract includes the lungs and the large bronchial tubes, or bronchi, that connect them to the trachea. The lungs are the site at which oxygen is absorbed into the bloodstream and carbon dioxide is removed from it. Small sacs called alveoli line the lungs. The interior surface of the lung tissue is moist and permeable and dense with tiny blood vessels called capillaries, which allow for the exchange of gases.

The process of respiration begins when air enters the body through the nose or mouth and travels to the lungs through the larynx, trachea, and bronchi. The main stem bronchi, which branch off from the trachea and lead to the lungs, divide into smaller bronchi, which separate into even smaller tubes called bronchioles. The bronchioles end in the capillary-rich alveoli. Blood laden with carbon dioxide and other waste products collected from throughout the body is pumped by the heart to the lungs through the pulmonary artery. As this blood moves through the capillaries, carbon dioxide is released through the alveoli into the bronchioles and on toward the nose and mouth, where it is exhaled. The carbon dioxide is replaced in the bloodstream by oxygen, which is carried to the heart through the pulmonary veins.

Most of the airways that conduct oxygen and carbon dioxide to and from the alveoli are held permanently open by muscle or by bony or cartilaginous frameworks. A protective layer called the epithelium, which traps and removes contaminants such as dust, lines these passageways.

Reading Time _1:35_

Recalling Facts

1. During respiration, blood is enriched with _____ and cleansed of _____.
   - ❑ a. carbon dioxide; oxygen
   - ❑ b. oxygen; carbon dioxide
   - ❑ c. oxygen; carbon monoxide

2. The upper respiratory tract includes the
   - ❑ a. sinus spaces, larynx, and bronchi.
   - ❑ b. larynx, trachea, and bronchi.
   - ❑ c. sinus spaces, larynx, and trachea.

3. Alveoli are found
   - ❑ a. in the epithelium of the bronchi.
   - ❑ b. at the end of the bronchioles.
   - ❑ c. in the area of the ethmoid bone.

4. Oxygen enters the bloodstream through the _____ of the alveoli.
   - ❑ a. epithelium
   - ❑ b. ethmoid cells
   - ❑ c. capillaries

5. Most of the airways that conduct gases in the body are
   - ❑ a. always held open.
   - ❑ b. opened and closed by muscle action.
   - ❑ c. made of cartilage and bone.

Understanding Ideas

6. One can infer from the article that in the respiratory system,
   - ❑ a. the heart is the most important organ.
   - ❑ b. the brain is the most important organ.
   - ❑ c. the lungs are the most important organs.

7. The sense of smell
   - ❑ a. involves only the nose.
   - ❑ b. is unrelated to respiration.
   - ❑ c. is dependent to some extent on respiration.

8. When the alveoli wall is described as permeable, that means that
   - ❑ a. gas molecules pass through it easily.
   - ❑ b. it is an effective barrier.
   - ❑ c. contaminants get caught in it.

9. Which of these is *not* a correct inference?
   - ❑ a. Without expiration, some waste products would remain in the bloodstream.
   - ❑ b. The number of alveoli in the lungs is not important.
   - ❑ c. The movement of blood through the capillaries aids in the exchange of gases.

10. One could conclude from this article that
    - ❑ a. the respiratory system has more airways than it needs.
    - ❑ b. insufficient gas exchange is a sign of disease.
    - ❑ c. contaminants that are carried to the lungs cannot enter the bloodstream.

Taking Care of the Lungs

Healthy lungs are crucial to a person's physical well-being. According to the American Lung Association, more than 30 million people in the United States are living with chronic lung disease today. Lung disease is the third leading cause of death in the United States. Lung damage often takes the form of fibrosis, a scarring of the lung walls that slows the flow of oxygen into the bloodstream, as well as the removal of carbon dioxide.

Chronic lung ailments linked with the workplace are known collectively as occupational lung diseases. Miners who breathe coal dust, construction workers exposed to asbestos or silica, and those in a variety of occupations who deal with hazardous chemicals can develop illnesses that do permanent damage to the lungs. Air pollution, including smog and elevated ozone levels caused by auto exhaust and power plant or factory emissions, is also detrimental to lung health.

The leading cause of lung disease—and of the complications that exacerbate lung disease—is cigarette smoking. Irritating gases and particles in tobacco smoke damage the cilia—tiny hairlike structures that line the bronchi. Cigarette smoking causes swelling in the lungs and also changes the enzyme balance, resulting in destruction of the lung tissue. Avoiding cigarette smoke is the single most effective action a person can take toward the preservation of good lung health.

(1 min)

1. Recognizing Words in Context

Find the word *exacerbate* in the passage. One definition below is closest in meaning to that word. One definition has the opposite or nearly opposite meaning. The remaining definition has a completely different meaning. Label the definitions C for *closest*, O for *opposite or nearly opposite*, and D for *different*.

_____ a. soothe

_____ b. eliminate

_____ c. aggravate

2. Distinguishing Fact from Opinion

Two of the statements below present *facts*, which can be proved correct. The other statement is an *opinion*, which expresses someone's thoughts or beliefs. Label the statements F for *fact* and O for *opinion*.

_____ a. Cigarette smoking does not benefit the lungs.

_____ b. Several occupations are associated with chronic lung disease.

_____ c. Healthy lungs are the most important aspect of good health.

3. Keeping Events in Order

Label the statements below 1, 2, and 3 to show the order in which the events happen.

_____ a. Gases begin to damage the cilia.

_____ b. Fibrosis impedes diffusion of oxygen into the blood stream.

_____ c. A person smokes cigarettes.

4. Making Correct Inferences

Two of the statements below are correct *inferences*, or reasonable guesses. They are based on information in the passage. The other statement is an incorrect, or faulty, inference. Label the statements C for *correct* inference and F for *faulty* inference.

_____ a. A reduced level of oxygen in the bloodstream harms the function of other organs.

_____ b. All lung damage is permanent.

_____ c. People who smoke can improve their lung function if they quit.

5. Understanding Main Ideas

One of the statements below expresses the main idea of the passage. One statement is too general, or too broad. The other explains only part of the passage; it is too narrow. Label the statements M for *main idea*, B for *too broad*, and N for *too narrow*.

_____ a. Coal miners are susceptible to lung disease.

_____ b. Leading causes of death include heart disease, cancer, and lung disease.

_____ c. Workplace contaminants, air pollution, and smoking cause lung disease.

Correct Answers, Part A _____7_____

Correct Answers, Part B _____

Total Correct Answers _____

Antarctica, the ice-shrouded continent encircling the South Pole, is remote and inhospitable. It is Earth's coldest, driest, and windiest place. The lowest temperature ever recorded there is −89°C (−129°F), and winds often reach 320 kilometers (200 miles) per hour.

Despite a climate so harsh that no land-dwelling vertebrate animals reside on the continent, Antarctica is surrounded by an ocean in which life is abundant. Plankton, the tiny plants and animals that drift in water, are the foundation of the marine food chain. Among the important plankton organisms are krill—small, shrimplike crustaceans that swarm around the ice floes and feed on algae. Many varieties of fish and marine mammals depend on krill for food.

About 200 kinds of fish inhabit the Antarctic waters, most of which are bottom-dwellers like the Antarctic cod, eel-pouts, and icefish. Hagfish, barracuda, lantern fish, and skates also make their homes in these cold waters. The largest Antarctic creatures, however, are seals and birds.

Weddell, Ross, crabeater, and leopard seals are native to the continent, and elephant and fur seals are occasional visitors. Each of the species has a different diet or frequents a different region of Antarctica, so the species rarely compete for resources. Seals were, however, the first Antarctic animals to be commercially hunted, and by the 1820s several species were close to extinction.

Among the most prominent denizens of Antarctica is the penguin, a gregarious, flightless bird that lives and breeds in colonies on the pack ice and the coast. Thought by early Antarctic explorers to be fish, penguins are superb swimmers that feed on fish, cuttlefish, crustaceans, and various other small sea animals. Their natural enemies include leopard seals, killer whales, and predatory birds like the skua, which feeds on penguin eggs and chicks. The best-known penguin of Antarctica—the Emperor penguin—is also the world's largest. In addition to penguins, some 35 species of seabirds live in Antarctica, although only 18 of these breed on the continent itself. The albatross and the petrel range far out to sea in search of food, while cormorants, terns, and sheathbills forage close to shore.

Although whales are not regular residents of the waters around the pack ice, a number of species, including blue, humpback, Southern right, and sperm whales, as well as killer whales, search the area for food in the spring. Occasionally minke whales and Southern bottlenosed whales are spotted there during the winter.

Reading Time ___2 min___

Recalling Facts

1. Antarctica is the only continent
   - ❏ a. surrounded by oceans.
   - ❏ b. with a harsh climate.
   - ❏ c. uninhabited by land-dwelling vertebrates.

2. _____ form the foundation of the marine food chain in Antarctica.
   - ❏ a. Plankton
   - ❏ b. Fish
   - ❏ c. Penguins

3. Which of the following seals is *not* native to Antarctica?
   - ❏ a. Ross seal
   - ❏ b. elephant seal
   - ❏ c. leopard seal

4. The first explorers to arrive in Antarctica thought penguins were
   - ❏ a. birds.
   - ❏ b. fish.
   - ❏ c. seals.

5. Whales search the Antarctic waters for food
   - ❏ a. primarily in the warmer months.
   - ❏ b. only in the winter.
   - ❏ c. throughout the year.

Understanding Ideas

6. One may conclude that
   - ❏ a. temperatures on Antarctica are only occasionally below freezing.
   - ❏ b. the Antarctic landmass abounds with many forms of animal life.
   - ❏ c. research scientists must have special resources to survive on Antarctica.

7. One may conclude that plankton are important to the marine food chain because
   - ❏ a. only tiny fish feed on them.
   - ❏ b. they are among the smallest and most abundant life forms in the oceans.
   - ❏ c. Southern right whales depend on them for nourishment.

8. The first people to visit Antarctica on a regular basis were probably
   - ❏ a. naturalists trying to protect animals from extinction.
   - ❏ b. tourists who wanted to see penguins.
   - ❏ c. hunters looking for seals.

9. Which of the following is true?
   - ❏ a. Marine mammals present no great danger to adult penguins.
   - ❏ b. A penguin cannot properly be termed a seabird.
   - ❏ c. About three dozen species of seabirds breed in Antarctica.

10. One may conclude from this article that _____ are the most common life form in Antarctica.
    - ❏ a. fish
    - ❏ b. birds
    - ❏ c. mammals

Icebergs of the Arctic Ocean

The glistening, aquamarine icebergs floating in the Arctic Ocean range from the size of a small car to that of a 10-story skyscraper. Whatever its magnitude, however, most of an iceberg's bulk is hidden beneath the ocean's surface. The base of an iceberg can extend so deep that it cuts grooves called ice scours into the seafloor; it can even get stuck in mud there. Since icebergs lie mostly underwater, currents affect them more than the wind does.

An iceberg is created through a process called calving. As a glacier or an ice cap expands into the sea, it is hammered by the movement of the tides, accentuated by the waves and weather. Erosion and the stress of the pounding water fracture the ice where it is weakest, and eventually a chunk floats free as an iceberg.

The Greenland ice cap produces most of the Arctic's icebergs; a few originate from the glaciers on islands around Baffin Bay, west of Greenland. At any given time, Arctic currents are propelling as many as 10,000 icebergs in a southerly direction, through the Davis Strait and into the open waters of the Atlantic Ocean. As the water temperature begins to rise in the lower latitudes, the icebergs melt; only a gargantuan iceberg will stay intact long enough to complete the two- to three-year journey to the Grand Banks off Newfoundland. In 1912, it was just such an immense iceberg that ripped through the hull of the *Titanic* on her maiden voyage.

1. **Recognizing Words in Context**

   Find the word *gargantuan* in the passage. One definition below is closest to the meaning of that word. One definition has the opposite or nearly opposite meaning. The remaining definition has a completely different meaning. Label the definitions C for *closest*, O for *opposite or nearly opposite*, and D for *different*.

   _____ a. miniature

   _____ b. immense

   _____ c. sharp

2. **Distinguishing Fact from Opinion**

   Two of the statements below present *facts*, which can be proved correct. The other statement is an *opinion*, which expresses someone's thoughts or beliefs. Label the statements F for *fact* and O for *opinion*.

   _____ a. Some of the icebergs in the Arctic Ocean are much larger than others.

   _____ b. Some Arctic icebergs originate from glaciers on the islands of Baffin Bay.

   _____ c. Icebergs are the greatest danger a ship captain faces.

3. Keeping Events in Order

Label the statements below 1, 2, and 3 to show the order in which the events happen.

_____ a. Glaciers grow and extend out into the sea.

_____ b. Pounding waves fracture the ice.

_____ c. Icebergs melt as they travel into southerly waters.

4. Making Correct Inferences

Two of the statements below are correct *inferences,* or reasonable guesses. They are based on information in the passage. The other statement is an incorrect, or faulty, inference. Label the statements C for *correct* inference and F for *faulty* inference.

_____ a. An iceberg floating in the Atlantic Ocean near Newfoundland must originally have been extremely large.

_____ b. Most icebergs touch the bottom of the ocean at some point.

_____ c. All icebergs come from glaciers or ice caps.

5. Understanding Main Ideas

One of the statements below expresses the main idea of the passage. One statement is too general, or too broad. The other explains only part of the passage; it is too narrow. Label the statements M for *main idea,* B for *too broad,* and N for *too narrow.*

_____ a. Most arctic icebergs break off of the Greenland ice cap and float south.

_____ b. Parts of some ice caps spread into the sea and break up.

_____ c. Arctic icebergs that float into the warmer waters of the Atlantic are a hazard to ships.

Correct Answers, Part A _____

Correct Answers, Part B _____

Total Correct Answers _____

18 A Bats

There are nearly 1,000 bat species in existence, more than any other kind of mammal species—and bats are the only mammals that can fly. Bats range in size from the bumblebee-sized Kitti's hog-nosed bat to the Malayan flying fox, whose wingspan can extend to almost 1.8 meters (6 feet).

Most bats eschew sunshine, preferring to forage in the shadowy light of dawn and dusk or under cover of darkness. Bats consume a variety of foods, including flower nectars, fruits, insects, small animals, and fish. They are natural enemies of nocturnal insect pests and important pollinators of at least 500 species of plants. Their waste material, guano, is a nitrogen-rich fertilizer. Bats' predators include snakes, hawks, owls, weasels, raccoons, wild and domestic dogs, and cats.

Living in almost every part of the world, from the cold, treeless plains of northern Canada to the humid tropical rain forests of Borneo, bats favor habitats that provide them with abundant food supplies and numerous places to roost. Although some species of bats are solitary, most live in colonies that can number from the hundreds to the millions. During the day, bats rest hanging upside down, enfolded in their wings of skin. Some bats roost in enclosed spaces such as caves and tree cavities; others hang in the open air from tree limbs or artificial structures. Maintaining this hanging position is effortless: the bat's weight causes its foot tendons to contract automatically and keep it firmly attached to its roost. Caves and mines offer excellent shelter for bats, providing innumerable footholds, protection from rain, wind, and extreme temperatures, and a secure place for raising young.

Nevertheless, bat populations are declining rapidly worldwide through loss of habitat. Human population growth has resulted in the loss of many bats' feeding and roosting areas. An irrational fear of bats, rooted in myths and folktales, has also led to efforts by some people to exterminate whole colonies.

But there is hope. In the United States, nearly 40 percent of native bat species either are currently protected under the federal Endangered Species Act or are candidates for protection. In 1980, repairs under the Congress Avenue Bridge in Austin, Texas, inadvertently created welcoming roosts for more than a million Mexican free-tailed bats. Initially resistant to the bats' presence, citizens came to welcome the colony, which has since become a tourist attraction. The city has built other structures that provide habitats for bats.

Reading Time _____ 2 min

Recalling Facts

1. Kitti's hog-nosed bat is about the size of a
   - ❏ a. bumblebee.
   - ❏ b. rat.
   - ❏ c. fox.

2. Most bats
   - ❏ a. forage on flower nectar and fruit.
   - ❏ b. sleep during daylight hours.
   - ❏ c. live in caves.

3. Bats prefer to live in
   - ❏ a. cool environments.
   - ❏ b. tropical rain forests.
   - ❏ c. locations that provide many places to roost.

4. A group of bats living in the same place is called a
   - ❏ a. colony.
   - ❏ b. flock.
   - ❏ c. swarm.

5. Which of the following represents the greatest threat to bat populations?
   - ❏ a. natural predators
   - ❏ b. people
   - ❏ c. disease

Understanding Ideas

6. One could conclude from this article that
   - ❏ a. bats threaten to destroy entire fruit crops.
   - ❏ b. bats become sick in sunlight.
   - ❏ c. there is considerable variety in bat species.

7. Which of the following inferences is most likely correct?
   - ❏ a. Bats use little energy clinging to their roosts.
   - ❏ b. Bats have very weak tendons in their feet.
   - ❏ c. Bats weigh a lot for their size.

8. Ideas about bats that come from myths and folktales
   - ❏ a. are almost always true.
   - ❏ b. are generally not supported by science.
   - ❏ c. help scientists protect endangered species of bats.

9. One could conclude from this article that bats
   - ❏ a. serve no use to people who live in cities.
   - ❏ b. create problems for miners.
   - ❏ c. provide many benefits to farmers.

10. The best time of day to see bats flying about is probably
    - ❏ a. an hour after sunrise.
    - ❏ b. just after sunset.
    - ❏ c. a few hours before sunset.

For bat fanciers and cavers alike, one of the most fascinating places to encounter and enjoy animal life and geological forms is Carlsbad Caverns National Park in New Mexico.

A century ago, a young man named Jim White, carrying a lamp he had made from a coffeepot, explored the subterranean depths of a guano mine and told tales of soaring white columns and glistening pools. By 1915 tourists could ride a bucket "elevator" 170 feet down to experience these wonders for themselves. In 1923 President Calvin Coolidge authorized the creation of the Carlsbad Cave National Monument, and seven years later Congress expanded it to Carlsbad Caverns National Park.

The caverns were created some 250,000,000 years ago as naturally occurring and corrosive sulfuric acid dissolved solid limestone. About 500,000 years ago, calcium carbonate that was dissolved in water dripping and seeping throughout the caverns produced stalagmites that rise up from the ground and stalactites that hang like icicles from the ceiling. Pale and luminous in the artificial light, these marvelous formations are found in many of the 83 caves and 50 kilometers (30 miles) of passages.

A million Mexican free-tailed bats make their summer home and raise their babies in a passageway near the entrance to the caves. At sunset, a black whirlwind spirals outward; it can take up to two hours for the last bat to emerge. They gorge themselves on night-flying insects along the Pecos and Black rivers and return at dawn individually or in small groups.

1. **Recognizing Words in Context**

   Find the word *subterranean* in the passage. One definition below is closest to the meaning of that word. One definition has the opposite or nearly opposite meaning. The remaining definition has a completely different meaning. Label the definitions C for *closest*, O for *opposite or nearly opposite*, and D for *different*.

   _____ a. underground

   _____ b. marine

   _____ c. celestial

2. **Distinguishing Fact from Opinion**

   Two of the statements below present *facts*, which can be proved correct. The other statement is an *opinion*, which expresses someone's thoughts or beliefs. Label the statements F for *fact* and O for *opinion*.

   _____ a. The Carlsbad Caverns are about 250 million years old.

   _____ b. The formations in the Carlsbad Caverns are a marvel.

   _____ c. Stalactites resemble icicles.

3. Keeping Events in Order

Label the statements below 1, 2, and 3 to show the order in which the events happen.

_____ a. Water full of dissolved calcium and other minerals seeps into the caves.

_____ b. Stalagmites grow in different formations from the floor of the caves.

_____ c. Sulfuric acid dissolves whole sections of solid limestone.

4. Making Correct Inferences

Two of the statements below are correct *inferences,* or reasonable guesses. They are based on information in the passage. The other statement is an incorrect, or faulty, inference. Label the statements C for *correct* inference and F for *faulty* inference.

_____ a. Mexican free-tailed bats fly south in the fall.

_____ b. Among the first people to regularly visit the caverns were guano miners.

_____ c. One could easily become lost in Carlsbad Caverns.

5. Understanding Main Ideas

One of the statements below expresses the main idea of the passage. One statement is too general, or too broad. The other explains only part of the passage; it is too narrow. Label the statements M for *main idea,* B for *too broad,* and N for *too narrow.*

_____ a. Bats and mineral formations are attractions at the Carlsbad Caverns National Park.

_____ b. Amazing caves can be visited in New Mexico and Kentucky.

_____ c. Carlsbad Caverns contains stalactites and stalagmites.

Correct Answers, Part A _____

Correct Answers, Part B _____

Total Correct Answers _____

Rain Forests

Rain forests, found in Earth's temperate and tropical zones, are some of the most biologically diverse ecosystems on the planet. Though currently accounting for less than 7 percent of Earth's surface, rain forests are estimated by scientists to contain well over half of the world's known plant and animal species. Most rain forests are located within the tropical band on either side of the equator, in South and Central America, Central Africa, and Southeast Asia. Large temperate rain forests can be found in the northwestern United States and in southwestern Canada near the coast of the Pacific Ocean.

All rain forests share certain distinctive features, including a closed canopy, a humid climate, and relatively uniform temperatures throughout the year. From the air, the forest canopy—the impenetrable foliage of the uppermost branches that forms a roof above the forest floor—is a solid mass of greenery. Most of the forest's insect and animal life flourishes in the canopy's leafy and sunlit environment. The forest's undergrowth, by comparison, is meager. Less than 2 percent of the sun's light penetrates the canopy and the darkness below. This darkness, along with the poor quality of the soils, hampers plant growth. Annual rainfall in rain forests ranges from about 200 to 1000 centimeters (80 inches to 400 inches) a year. Temperatures in tropical rain forests often hover around 27°C (80°F).

Rain forests are an essential component of Earth's total ecology. Huge amounts of water are absorbed into tree roots and recycled into the atmosphere from the trees' leaves through a process called transpiration. Tree roots also anchor the soil in place and slow the runoff of rains into rivers and oceans. Through the process of photosynthesis, rain forests absorb more carbon dioxide and give off more oxygen than any other ecosystem.

Unfortunately, the rain forests are shrinking at a rapid rate as a result of the profitable ventures of ranching, logging, and mining. When tropical rain forests are cleared in order to raise cattle and crops, the nutrient-poor soils quickly wear out. When farmers move on to new areas, torrential rains and blazing sun leave the land sterile and lifeless. Logging and mining cause similar damage to the land and destroy the habitat of untold millions of birds, animals, insects, and reptiles. By some estimates, an area of tropical rain forest the size of the state of Delaware disappears in this way every month.

Recalling Facts

1. Rain forests account for about
   _____ of Earth's land surface.
   - ❑ a. 55 percent
   - ❑ b. 27 percent
   - ❑ c. 7 percent

2. Which of the following is *not* a
   feature of a tropical rain forest?
   - ❑ a. moist climate
   - ❑ b. nutrient-rich soils
   - ❑ c. uniform temperatures

3. Most of a rain forest's animal and
   insect life lives
   - ❑ a. in the canopy.
   - ❑ b. on the forest floor.
   - ❑ c. at the edges of the forest.

4. Rain forests are especially valuable
   for their production of
   - ❑ a. carbon dioxide.
   - ❑ b. ozone.
   - ❑ c. oxygen.

5. Earth's rain forests are
   - ❑ a. shrinking at a rapid rate.
   - ❑ b. are growing larger constantly.
   - ❑ c. the same size as they always
     have been.

Understanding Ideas

6. One may conclude from this article
   that rain forests
   - ❑ a. are important mainly to the
     people who live there.
   - ❑ b. contribute to the ecological
     health of the planet.
   - ❑ c. cannot survive with such poor
     quality soil.

7. The concentration of animal and
   insect life in the canopy suggests that
   - ❑ a. most animals and insects need
     sunlight in order to thrive.
   - ❑ b. they are safe from predators
     there.
   - ❑ c. it is cold on the forest floor.

8. Many people believe that _____
   represents the most significant threat
   to the survival of rain forests.
   - ❑ a. the blazing sun
   - ❑ b. erosion from torrential rains
   - ❑ c. human activity

9. It is important to preserve the rain
   forests because they
   - ❑ a. are home to vast numbers of
     plant and animal species.
   - ❑ b. can't be used for anything else.
   - ❑ c. protect the land until it can be
     farmed.

10. One can conclude that
    - ❑ a. birds and animals displaced
      from the rain forest can live
      elsewhere.
    - ❑ b. rain forests are easily regrown
      after the trees are cleared.
    - ❑ c. some people are more concerned
      with earning a living than with
      protecting the environment.

Saving the Rain Forest

As the world's rain forests continue to shrink, future generations are losing more than the beauties of these regions. Modern medical research conducted in gleaming laboratories owes much to the rain forest—to its resources and to the shamans who preserve the wisdom of the ethnic groups that live there. The destruction of the rain forests has caused the extinction of countless plant, animal, and insect species. This damage may also prevent or delay us from finding cures for many life-threatening diseases, such as cancer.

In the 17th century, the Spanish learned from the Peruvians how to treat malaria with the bark of the quinine tree. The rain forests also gave us treatments for arthritis, diabetes, and glaucoma. In fact, one quarter of the prescription drugs sold today use ingredients from the rain forest.

It is not only the plants and the animals of the rain forest that are endangered, but also its indigenous peoples. When European colonists arrived in the Americas about 500 years ago, for instance, perhaps 10 million natives lived in the Amazon River basin rain forest. Now, fewer than 200,000 of their descendents survive. As the tribes and their shamans vanish, so too does their unique knowledge of local plants and the remedies they provide.

1. **Recognizing Words in Context**

   Find the word *indigenous* in the passage. One definition below is closest to the meaning of that word. One definition has the opposite or nearly opposite meaning. The remaining definition has a completely different meaning. Label the definitions C for *closest*, O for *opposite or nearly opposite,* and D for *different.*

   _____ a. rigorous

   _____ b. alien

   _____ c. native

2. **Distinguishing Fact from Opinion**

   Two of the statements below present *facts,* which can be proved correct. The other statement is an *opinion,* which expresses someone's thoughts or beliefs. Label the statements F for *fact* and O for *opinion.*

   _____ a. Scientists are more important than shamans.

   _____ b. Shamans have devised remedies from the resources of the rain forest.

   _____ c. Scientists cannot learn about the medical properties of some rain forest resources without the help of the shamans.

3. Keeping Events in Order

Label the statements below 1, 2, and 3 to show the order in which the events happen.

_____ a. The Spanish begin to use quinine tree bark to treat malaria.

_____ b. European colonists settle in the Americas.

_____ c. About 200,000 members of tribes indigenous to the Amazonian rain forest survive.

4. Making Correct Inferences

Two of the statements below are correct *inferences,* or reasonable guesses. They are based on information in the passage. The other statement is an incorrect, or faulty, inference. Label the statements C for *correct* inference and F for *faulty* inference.

_____ a. Tribal shamans were using the medical properties of certain plants long before these cures were discovered by scientists.

_____ b. If the rain forests disappear, the land will be turned to some other equally valuable use.

_____ c. Traditional lore and scientific research can both contribute to medical discoveries.

5. Understanding Main Ideas

One of the statements below expresses the main idea of the passage. One statement is too general, or too broad. The other explains only part of the passage; it is too narrow. Label the statements M for *main idea,* B for *too broad,* and N for *too narrow.*

_____ a. Diseases such as malaria and glaucoma can be controlled with drugs made from rain forest plants.

_____ b. Many plant and animal species are endangered.

_____ c. The rain forest is an important resource for modern medical research.

Correct Answers, Part A ___10___ (2nd reading)

Correct Answers, Part B ___15___

Total Correct Answers ___25___

A genome is the complete set of deoxyribonucleic acid (DNA) in an organism. DNA—the chainlike molecule found in the nuclei of all cells—contains the genetic coded data that determine the characteristics of each individual organism and make it unique. Sequences of DNA containing information about specific inherited traits are called genes and are carried on structures called chromosomes. Human beings normally have 23 pairs of chromosomes.

Scientists have determined that a person's genes hold the answers to many questions about life and health. If a gene causing a certain sickness can be located on a particular chromosome, for instance, then researchers can focus on that gene in an effort to prevent or cure the illness. If an illness is inherited, then it may be possible one day to repair the gene itself, curing the disease in one person and halting the spread of it to subsequent generations.

The U.S. Department of Energy and the National Institutes of Health have overseen the Human Genome Project (HGP), which was founded in 1990. The HGP is an effort to "map" the genetic matter shared by all human beings. Scientists have focused on identifying what many think are about 30,000 genes in human DNA. They have also established the sequence of the 3 billion chemical base pairs that make up human DNA. By June 2000 the map had been sketched out; analyses of those early results were published in February 2001. There are five main locations where this research is ongoing, and dozens of public and private organizations around the world are also engaged in genetic and genomic research.

The HGP has taken on more than just the detailed mapping of the human genome. Its discoveries are likely to affect all aspects of human health and the way people look at sickness, aging, and human potential. The project has wide economic implications as well. The facts compiled from research will be stored in databases, and more advanced tools will be developed to analyze the data. The government plans to license new technologies that emerge from the project to private businesses in order to strengthen the U.S. biotechnology industry and to foster the creation of new medical treatments. The project is not without controversy, however. Some people are concerned that findings from the HGP will be used to develop products and treatments before sufficient testing has been done to determine potential dangers.

Reading Time 1:45

Recalling Facts

1. A genome is
   - ❏ a. only the complete set of DNA in a human.
   - ❏ b. the complete set of DNA in any organism.
   - ❏ c. the number of chromosomes in an organism.

2. Genes are made of _____ and located _____.
   - ❏ a. chromosomes; on the DNA
   - ❏ b. DNA; in the walls of cells
   - ❏ c. DNA; on the chromosomes

3. The Human Genome Project is under the supervision of
   - ❏ a. both public and private organizations.
   - ❏ b. the biotechnology industry.
   - ❏ c. the U.S. government.

4. Which of the following statements is *not* true?
   - ❏ a. The HGP's only task is to map the human genome.
   - ❏ b. The National Institutes of Health is involved in the HGP.
   - ❏ c. The work of the HGP is an ongoing project conducted at five main sites.

5. There are about _____ genes in human DNA.
   - ❏ a. 23 pairs of
   - ❏ b. 3 billion
   - ❏ c. 30,000

Understanding Ideas

6. One could conclude that
   - ❏ a. the organization of the human genome is easy to determine.
   - ❏ b. scientists do not know exactly how many genes are in the human genome.
   - ❏ c. scientists have used traditional technology for this project.

7. One can infer that a person's DNA
   - ❏ a. is unique.
   - ❏ b. matches that of his or her mother and father.
   - ❏ c. matches that of his or her brothers and sisters.

8. Which inference is correct?
   - ❏ a. Many bankers and economists also work for the HGP.
   - ❏ b. Medical researchers make up a key part of the HGP staff.
   - ❏ c. All of the people who work for the HGP also work for the U.S. government.

9. To eliminate a hereditary illness, doctors would need to
   - ❏ a. eliminate all chromosomes.
   - ❏ b. completely replace a person's DNA.
   - ❏ c. locate the gene that is associated with the illness.

10. One could conclude that
    - ❏ a. governments will closely monitor the way that companies use the HGP research.
    - ❏ b. governments will give companies complete freedom in their use of HGP research.
    - ❏ c. governments will halt further HGP research.

Ethics and the Human Genome Project

Since the Human Genome Project (HGP) was founded in 1990, three to five percent of the project's budget has been given each year to its bioethics program. The bioethics program examines the various human issues raised by the dissemination of genetic information. It also addresses the issue of whether the project is a good use of taxpayers' money.

Some scientists fear that wasteful spending by HGP managers diverts funding from other research programs. They worry that the glamour of a "big science" project such as mapping the human genome will outshine "small science" efforts that are likely to yield new medical treatments.

People have raised many other questions about the impact of gene research. For example, what would happen if someone carrying a gene for a hereditary disease wanted to buy health insurance? It is foreseeable that an insurance company might charge higher rates or even deny coverage to healthy people who have such a gene even if they have not developed the disease.

What impact would genetic information have on the ways people treat illness, care for the elderly, and plan families? Will various interpretations of genetic information affect the laws the government enacts, the services it offers, or the development of foreign and domestic policy? These are some of the ethical issues being raised.

1. **Recognizing Words in Context**

   Find the word *dissemination* in the passage. One definition below is closest to the meaning of that word. One has the opposite or nearly opposite meaning. The remaining definition has a completely different meaning. Label the definitions C for *closest,* O for *opposite or nearly opposite,* and D for *different.*

   _____ a. restriction

   _____ b. distribution

   _____ c. hostility

2. **Distinguishing Fact from Opinion**

   Two of the statements below present facts, which can be proved correct. The other statement is an opinion, which expresses someone's thoughts or beliefs. Label the statements F for *fact* and O for *opinion.*

   _____ a. The HGP is a worthy way to spend the taxpayers' money.

   _____ b. Bioethics examines the impact of science on human issues.

   _____ c. The HGP is a large and complex project that deals with issues related to genetics.

3. Keeping Events in Order

Label the statements below 1, 2, and 3 to show the order in which the events happen.

_____ a. A woman decides to be tested for a gene linked to Alzheimer's disease.

_____ b. Two of a woman's grandparents die from Alzheimer's disease.

_____ c. A gene linked to Alzheimer's disease is located in a woman's chromosomes.

4. Making Correct Inferences

Two of the statements below are correct *inferences*, or reasonable guesses. They are based on information in the passage. The other statement is an incorrect, or faulty, inference. Label the statements C for *correct* inference and F for *faulty* inference.

_____ a. Making genetic information widely available is likely to have an impact on the economy.

_____ b. Not everyone agrees on the value of the HGP.

_____ c. Most married couples who know what genes they have will decide not to have children.

5. Understanding Main Ideas

One of the statements below expresses the main idea of the passage. One statement is too general, or too broad. The other explains only part of the passage; it is too narrow. Label the statements M for *main idea*, B for *too broad*, and N for *too narrow*.

_____ a. The HGP provides a wide range of information about genetics.

_____ b. Data from the HGP may affect the cost of health insurance.

_____ c. The study of bioethical issues is a component of the HGP.

Correct Answers, Part A ___8___

Correct Answers, Part B _____

Total Correct Answers _____

92

A dictionary might define physics as the scientific study of matter and energy and the interactions between the two. Physics has several different branches, including thermodynamics, acoustics, and mechanics. Thermodynamics involves heat, acoustics involves sound, and mechanics involves the forces that move things.

But what does physics have to do with the lives of ordinary people? Physics is also the process by which one can explain how things work, why things work, and often, why things don't work the way people want them to.

The first law of thermodynamics states that energy can never be created or destroyed but can only be transformed from one form into another. This helps to explain why standard light bulbs, called incandescent bulbs, are inefficient. In an incandescent bulb, electricity runs through a metal filament. To create light, the electricity must first create heat energy in the filament; when the filament becomes white hot, some of the heat energy is changed into light energy. Most of the energy is wasted as unneeded heat.

Physics also helps explain why traffic jams happen during rush hour on highways when there are no accidents or other obstructions. A few physicists at the Los Alamos National Laboratories in New Mexico put their computers to work on the problem. They designed computer models of the highways in Dallas, Texas, and Portland, Oregon, and used the models to simulate rush hours. They filled their cyber-roads with about two million cyber-cars and told the computer where and when each driver goes to work, takes the kids to school, picks them up at the mall, and so on. The simulations accurately replicated real traffic patterns, and the physicists developed the principle of "congestion waves." According to this principle, each movement that a vehicle makes causes a reaction in the vehicles around it. When, for example, a car slows suddenly or changes lanes without warning, fear of crashing causes the drivers in nearby cars to react, usually by stomping on the brake. As these cars slow down, they cause the cars behind them to slow down even more, creating a giant ripple effect. The farther a car is from the one that started it all, the stronger the driver's reaction, and the greater the obstacle is to the cars that follow.

People will always have questions about why the world is the way it is, and physics will always help to provide the answers.

Reading Time 1:45

Recalling Facts

1. Physics is defined as the study of
   - ❑ a. matter and energy and their interrelation.
   - ❑ b. physical science.
   - ❑ c. thermodynamics.

2. Which of these subjects belong to the study of physics?
   - ❑ a. geology and acoustics
   - ❑ b. thermodynamics and botany
   - ❑ c. acoustics and mechanics

3. The first law of thermodynamics states that energy cannot be
   - ❑ a. created without matter.
   - ❑ b. created or destroyed but only transformed.
   - ❑ c. destroyed but only transformed into matter.

4. Which of the following leads to traffic jams when there is no accident or other obstruction?
   - ❑ a. congestion waves
   - ❑ b. construction delays
   - ❑ c. computer models

5. Physicists used a computer to _____ traffic patterns around Dallas, Texas, and Portland, Oregon.
   - ❑ a. change
   - ❑ b. explain
   - ❑ c. simulate

Understanding Ideas

6. From the article, a room in which several incandescent light bulbs are on would be _____ than a similar room with only one light bulb on.
   - ❑ a. slightly warmer
   - ❑ b. slightly cooler
   - ❑ c. more efficient

7. The incandescent bulb is _____ to produce light.
   - ❑ a. the best way
   - ❑ b. a wasteful way
   - ❑ c. the safest way

8. Which of the following problems is *least* likely to require the expertise of a physicist?
   - ❑ a. the way that hurricane winds damages buildings
   - ❑ b. the way that air pollution affects levels of solar radiation that reach Earth
   - ❑ c. the decline in the water quality of lakes and streams

9. One could conclude from this article that physicists
   - ❑ a. found a similarity between the ways that traffic and water move.
   - ❑ b. spend much of their time studying electricity and traffic.
   - ❑ c. found that each traffic jam happens in a unique way.

10. According to the first law of thermodynamics, there was _____ energy in the universe hundreds of millions of years ago.
    - ❑ a. more
    - ❑ b. the same amount of
    - ❑ c. less

The Physics of Tennis

Would you rather see blazing serves and brute strength, or a slower, often more strategic game? Different court surfaces—and different equipment— have a great effect on how tennis is played.

Aficionados of strategy might enjoy watching tennis played on clay courts, because the fine sand that coats a clay court helps players slide in and out of shots as though moving on tiny ball bearings. Unlike spherical ball bearings, however, grains of sand have edges and rounded-off points; a surface covered with ball bearings would be slippery, but the sand on a clay court can improve the speed and agility of the player. Sand also slows down the ball by sticking to the fabric, increasing the friction of the bounce and lessening the speed at which the ball is traveling. Clay courts also give finesse players a better opportunity to use their full repertoire of spins, slices, and volleys.

Some fans prefer hardcourt tennis for its lightning-fast serves and passing shots. The excitement of speed may soon be in reduced supply, however. The International Tennis Federation is considering increasing the size of the regulation tennis ball by about six percent, from 6.68 centimeters (2.63 inches) in diameter to 7.09 centimeters (2.79 inches). The larger surface area of the new ball would provide more air resistance, slowing the ball and giving a player more time to react to a shot or a serve.

1. **Recognizing Words in Context**

   Find the word *aficionados* in the passage. One definition below is closest to the meaning of that word. One has the opposite or nearly opposite meaning. The remaining definition has a completely different meaning. Label the definitions C for *closest,* O for *opposite or nearly opposite,* and D for *different.*

   _____ a. people interested in something

   _____ b. people bored by something

   _____ c. people participating in something

2. **Distinguishing Fact from Opinion**

   Two of the statements below present *facts,* which can be proved correct. The other statement is an *opinion,* which expresses someone's thoughts or beliefs. Label the statements F for *fact* and O for *opinion.*

   _____ a. A tennis ball slows down when it hits the surface of a clay court.

   _____ b. Each player should be able to decide on the size of the ball he or she wants to use.

   _____ c. Some players perform better on grass courts.

3. Keeping Events in Order

Label the statements below 1, 2, and 3 to show the order in which the events happen.

_____ a. Finesse players begin to win more tournaments.

_____ b. Professional players who hit the hardest shots are dominating tennis.

_____ c. The International Tennis Federation decides to increase the size of the tennis ball.

4. Making Correct Inferences

Two of the statements below are correct *inferences,* or reasonable guesses. They are based on information in the passage. The other statement is an incorrect, or faulty, inference. Label the statements C for *correct* inference and F for *faulty* inference.

_____ a. Tennis played on grass courts is a completely different game than tennis played on clay courts is.

_____ b. The International Tennis Federation seeks to increase the audience for tennis.

_____ c. Players who excel on some surfaces play less well on others.

5. Understanding Main Ideas

One of the statements below expresses the main idea of the passage. One statement is too general, or too broad. The other explains only part of the passage; it is too narrow. Label the statements M for *main idea,* B for *too broad,* and N for *too narrow.*

_____ a. Equipment as well as the court surface affects the style of tennis played.

_____ b. The International Tennis Federation may change equipment regulations in an effort to attract a larger audience.

_____ c. Tennis requires many different types of shots.

Correct Answers, Part A __9__

Correct Answers, Part B _____

Total Correct Answers _____

22 A The Development of Multimedia

The term *multimedia* is derived from the root word *medium*, defined as "a means of expression." Painting is a medium in the visual arts, dance is a medium of performance, and words are the medium of poetry. *Medium* also can refer to something that comes in the middle. The medium as a means of expression is that which comes between the source of the message and the person who receives it.

The plural form *media* is often used to refer to newspapers, magazines, radio, and television. But in its broadest sense, *media* also incorporates literature, the fine arts, and even the Internet. The word *multimedia* first appeared in the 1960s to describe the simultaneous use of more than one medium. Early forms of multimedia included slide presentations accompanied by music.

Today's multimedia is much more sophisticated. A multimedia artist brings together sculpture, performance, light, and sound to create complex art. The term also applies to the world of the personal computer. It describes any computer presentation that combines text, graphics, full-motion video, and sound into a single package. Multimedia elements—on Web sites, on compact discs and DVDs, and even in e-mail programs—may also be interactive. Hyperlinks allow people to switch between topics, add sound and motion, and leap from idea to idea, making connections that they might not make when reading a book or watching television. Interactive users are not just spectators absorbing information in a predetermined sequence. They can map out a personal path through a world of content and experiences in such multimedia productions as games, special-interest Web sites, sales presentations, and encyclopedias.

In its essence, multimedia is not new, of course. The idea that one can express a thought using an integrated structure of diverse media is as old as humanity itself. Throughout history, cultures worldwide have combined the visual arts, music, dance, speech, architecture, and other elements to create their performances and rituals. Nor is the idea of direct participation in such events new. Religious ceremonies have long included participation by worshippers in the reading of texts and the singing of hymns. What is novel in the 21st century is the extent to which the computer enables people to pursue knowledge, explore new ideas, and create delightful sensory experiences, all on their own or in collaboration with others. For many, multimedia technology has become an integral part of daily life—at home, at school, and at work.

Reading Time 1:45

Recalling Facts

1. *Multimedia* refers to
   - ❏ a. the opportunity to use many different media.
   - ❏ b. the combining of different media in one project.
   - ❏ c. the use of different media in different projects.

2. The word *multimedia* came into use
   - ❏ a. in the 1950s.
   - ❏ b. in the 1960s.
   - ❏ c. in the 1970s.

3. Interactive features of multimedia programs
   - ❏ a. encourage users of the programs to be spectators.
   - ❏ b. limit the amount of information the programs can contain.
   - ❏ c. allow users to control the way they use the programs.

4. Which of the following is *not* true of multimedia forms of expression?
   - ❏ a. They first became possible with advances in computer technology.
   - ❏ b. They have appeared around the world throughout history.
   - ❏ c. They can include both sound and visual images.

5. Which of the following is *not* a meaning of *media*?
   - ❏ a. more than one medium
   - ❏ b. instruments of communication
   - ❏ c. the artistic experience

Understanding Ideas

6. An example of a medium is
   - ❏ a. an idea.
   - ❏ b. a billboard.
   - ❏ c. a news reporter.

7. A medium is
   - ❏ a. the reason for expressing a message in a certain way.
   - ❏ b. the way in which a message is expressed.
   - ❏ c. something that a person uses to express a message.

8. An example of a multimedia presentation would be
   - ❏ a. a poetry reading in which the reader conveyed a great deal of emotion.
   - ❏ b. a sculpture placed in front of a large video screen onto which photographs are projected.
   - ❏ c. an album containing photographs of many different places and people.

9. Which of the following could you most likely do on a computer by following a hyperlink?
   - ❏ a. make an outline of information in an article
   - ❏ b. open a word-processing program
   - ❏ c. switch from one topic to another

10. One could conclude from this article that interactive multimedia programs
    - ❏ a. discourage independent learning.
    - ❏ b. encourage independent learning.
    - ❏ c. are intended for small groups of users.

Reality is what people know to be true based on what their senses tell them. It could be said that reality is one's ongoing encounter with the world, combined with memories of the past. People can document reality. As one moves out of the present, however, the reality of the present becomes a memory, part of an unchanging past.

Virtual reality (VR) provides an illusion of solid, provable reality. Events that take place within VR, however, do not exist apart from reality.

Specifically, VR is a computer simulation that makes a person feel as if he or she is in a different environment, interacting with the forces that exist there. This VR might be modeled on reality; it could also be completely imaginary. VR's illusions are created through sights and sounds provided by a computer. Some of the most realistic effects are felt when the user dons headgear equipped with tiny television screens and wears special gloves, shoes, or clothing fitted with electronic sensors.

VR technology, which was developed during the 1980s, has been used for both entertainment and job training. Some of the simplest programs are computer games in which the player seems to move through fully three-dimensional space. VR can be used to train pilots and simulate unfamiliar sensations such as the weightlessness of space. VR may even be used one day to prepare medical students to be surgeons.

(1 min)

1. Recognizing Words in Context

Find the word *document* in the passage. One definition below is closest in meaning to that word. One definition as the opposite or nearly opposite meaning. The remaining definition has a completely different meaning. Label the definitions C for *closest*, O for *opposite or nearly opposite*, and D for *different*.

_____ a. read about

_____ b. support with evidence

_____ c. refute

2. Distinguishing Fact from Opinion

Two of the statements below present *facts*, which can be proved correct. The other statement is an *opinion*, which expresses someone's thoughts or beliefs. Label the statements F for *fact* and O for *opinion*.

_____ a. Environments in virtual reality seem real but are not.

_____ b. Advances in electronics contributed to the development of VR programs.

_____ c. Reality is more meaningful than virtual reality.

3. Keeping Events in Order

Label the statements below 1, 2, and 3 to show the order in which the events happen.

_____ a. A person uses a VR application that simulates space travel.

_____ b. A person participates in a space shuttle mission.

_____ c. A person begins an astronaut-training program.

4. Making Correct Inferences

Two of the statements below are correct *inferences*, or reasonable guesses. They are based on information in the passage. The other statement is an incorrect, or faulty, inference. Label the statements C for *correct* inference and F for *faulty* inference.

_____ a. When people use VR programs, their experiences are different from dreams.

_____ b. Virtual reality job training programs will one day be used in almost all professions.

_____ c. Many people know VR through their experiences with computer games.

5. Understanding Main Ideas

One of the statements below expresses the main idea of the passage. One statement is too general, or too broad. The other explains only part of the passage; it is too narrow. Label the statements M for *main idea*, B for *too broad*, and N for *too narrow*.

_____ a. Virtual reality technology is used in some forms of training.

_____ b. Computer simulations have grown more sophisticated over the years.

_____ c. Virtual reality replicates the experience of material reality.

Correct Answers, Part A ___7___

Correct Answers, Part B _____

Total Correct Answers _____

Potentially, any kind of matter can exist in three states—solid, liquid, or gas. The state that matter takes depends on several factors, the most important of which is temperature. Consider water: at room temperature, water is liquid. If the temperature falls to $0°C$ ($32°F$), water freezes and becomes solid. If the temperature rises to $100°C$ ($212°F$), water boils and becomes a gas. When a gas loses heat, it condenses and becomes liquid. When liquid matter gains heat, it evaporates and becomes gas.

Condensation and evaporation can happen slowly or quickly. The rate depends mainly on the temperature, because temperature is directly related to the kinetic energy of the molecules. Other factors involved in the rate of condensation or evaporation include the vapor pressure and the ductility of the matter. A higher vapor pressure causes a faster rate of evaporation. Sticky liquids have a higher ductility than water does, and so they evaporate more slowly.

During the process of condensation, the cooling of a gas causes it to lose the kinetic energy that keeps its molecules apart. The molecules move closer together until eventually the force of cohesion causes them to cling together, restricting their movement. At this point, the gas has condensed into a liquid. One of the most common examples of condensation is the water that forms on the exterior of a glass holding a chilled beverage. When the beverage is poured into a glass, it cools the glass. As the glass becomes colder than the surrounding air, it cools the air molecules with which it comes into contact. Water vapor in the air condenses into water droplets on the glass.

The process of evaporation is the reverse of condensation. When energy in the form of steady heat is applied to a liquid, the cohesion of the molecules is broken. As the molecules move apart, the tangible liquid becomes an intangible gas or vapor. The evaporation of a substance such as water requires very little energy. Water in a pan in a warm room evaporates into the air, though not as quickly as it does when it is placed in a pan on a hot stove.

People experience evaporation when they perspire. Perspiration, which is stimulated by sweat glands, absorbs heat from the body. As the kinetic energy of the perspiration increases, it begins to evaporate. This transfers heat from the body to the air and helps a person cool off.

Reading Time 1:40

Recalling Facts

1. The change of a liquid into a gas is called
   - ❏ a. condensation.
   - ❏ b. solidification.
   - ❏ c. evaporation.

2. Temperature is directly related to the _____ of molecules.
   - ❏ a. kinetic energy
   - ❏ b. potential energy
   - ❏ c. electromagnetic energy

3. _____ develops on the exterior of a glass holding a chilled beverage.
   - ❏ a. Evaporation
   - ❏ b. Condensation
   - ❏ c. Residue

4. When water vapor condenses, the molecules
   - ❏ a. are affected by the force of cohesion.
   - ❏ b. gain kinetic energy.
   - ❏ c. move farther apart.

5. Heating water _____ the rate of its evaporation.
   - ❏ a. slows
   - ❏ b. speeds
   - ❏ c. does not change

Understanding Ideas

6. It may take _____ to evaporate a substance that is solid at room temperature.
   - ❏ a. very low temperatures
   - ❏ b. just a moment
   - ❏ c. very high temperatures

7. According to the information in the article, which of the following contains the least kinetic energy?
   - ❏ a. ice
   - ❏ b. water
   - ❏ c. water vapor

8. From the article, which of the following might also be an example of condensation?
   - ❏ a. frost on the grass
   - ❏ b. dew on the grass
   - ❏ c. steam coming from a kettle

9. Liquid matter with low ductility would most likely evaporate
   - ❏ a. slowly.
   - ❏ b. rapidly.
   - ❏ c. not at all.

10. One could conclude from this article that condensation and evaporation of water
    - ❏ a. is an ongoing cycle.
    - ❏ b. stops in the winter.
    - ❏ c. cannot happen in a desert.

An Experiment: Distilling Water

Distilling water can remove dissolved minerals and contaminants, making the water pure and potable. This experiment in distillation requires the following materials: a large bowl, a small bowl, a sheet of plastic wrap, table salt, food coloring, a large coin, and ordinary tap water.

In the large bowl, combine about three cups of water, three tablespoons of salt, and a few drops of food coloring, making sure that the salt dissolves completely. Next, carefully place the smaller bowl inside the larger bowl without letting any water in. If the small bowl is unstable, try using a heavier small bowl or removing just enough water so that the smaller bowl rests steadily on the bottom of the larger bowl. Cover the larger bowl securely with the plastic wrap so that the sheet is flat but neither too taut nor too loose. Place the coin on top of the plastic near the center of the smaller bowl. Set the apparatus in a sunny, warm location. After a day or two, examine the smaller bowl. It will now contain water that neither tastes salty nor exhibits any color.

As the sun evaporated the tinted and salted water, the water vapor rose until it came into contact with the plastic wrap, where it condensed into droplets whose weight caused them to roll toward the coin. The condensation—distilled water—dripped into the smaller bowl.

(1·15)

1. **Recognizing Words in Context**

   Find the word *potable* in the passage. One definition below is closest to the meaning of that word. One definition has the opposite or nearly opposite meaning. The remaining definition has a completely different meaning. Label the definitions C for *closest,* O for *opposite or nearly opposite,* and D for *different.*

   _____ a. unfit for drinking

   _____ b. fit for drinking

   _____ c. enjoyable to drink

2. **Distinguishing Fact from Opinion**

   Two of the statements below present *facts,* which can be proved correct. The other statement is an *opinion,* which expresses someone's thoughts or beliefs. Label the statements F for *fact* and O for *opinion.*

   _____ a. When water is distilled properly, it will contain no dissolved minerals.

   _____ b. Properly distilled water is safe to drink.

   _____ c. Distilled water is the best water for drinking.

3. Keeping Events in Order

Label the statements below 1, 2, and 3 to show the order in which the steps should be performed.

_____ a. Examine and taste the contents of the small bowl.

_____ b. Set the small bowl inside the larger one.

_____ c. Mix water, salt, and food coloring in the large bowl.

4. Making Correct Inferences

Two of the statements below are correct *inferences,* or reasonable guesses. They are based on information in the passage. The other statement is an incorrect, or faulty, inference. Label the statements C for *correct* inference and F for *faulty* inference.

_____ a. It is safe to use any kind of water in this experiment.

_____ b. When the water evaporates, it leaves the salt and particles of color behind.

_____ c. Food coloring evaporates more slowly than water.

5. Understanding Main Ideas

One of the statements below expresses the main idea of the passage. One statement is too general, or too broad. The other explains only part of the passage; it is too narrow. Label the statements M for *main idea,* B for *too broad,* and N for *too narrow.*

_____ a. Distilling water rids it of dissolved substances.

_____ b. Water can be distilled by using two bowls and plastic wrap.

_____ c. Food coloring can help show that water has been distilled.

Correct Answers, Part A ___9___

Correct Answers, Part B _____

Total Correct Answers _____

Earth's atmosphere is composed of five distinct layers held in place by Earth's gravitational pull. The atmosphere is densest in the layers that are closest to Earth's surface: 99 percent of the atmosphere's mass is within 80 kilometers (50 miles) of the ground. This lower portion of the atmosphere is a uniform mixture of gases consisting of about 78 percent nitrogen, 21 percent oxygen, and 1 percent argon. Trace amounts of carbon dioxide, neon, helium, krypton, hydrogen, and ozone make up the rest. Close to Earth's surface, water vapor and pollutants are present in varying amounts. In the remaining 1 percent of the atmosphere, the proportions of lighter gases, such as hydrogen and helium, are somewhat higher.

The first layer of Earth's atmosphere, called the troposphere, is 8 kilometers (5 miles) high at the poles and 13 kilometers (8 miles) high at the equator. Mount Everest rises almost to the upper limit of the troposphere. The air of the troposphere is in constant motion, filled with horizontal and vertical air currents that create weather systems. Air pressure, normally about 101 kilopascals (14.7 pounds per square inch) at sea level, is only about 34 kilopascals (5 pounds per square inch) at the summit of Mount Everest. The temperature drops significantly as well.

The second layer of the atmosphere is called the stratosphere. It extends 32 kilometers (20 miles) beyond the troposphere, and its temperature is relatively constant. The air here also moves in strong horizontal currents. Next comes the mesosphere, the third layer, which is also about 32 kilometers thick. In this layer, temperatures drop sharply again, from about –2°C (28°F) at its lower levels to minus –110°C (–166°F) degrees at the top.

The fourth layer is the thermosphere. It is about 500 kilometers (310 miles) thick, and temperatures actually rise within this layer. The rapid increase in temperature is due to the absorption of short-wavelength radiation from the Sun. In the fifth and final layer, the exosphere, air density is so low that there is essentially no temperature at all. On average, an air molecule here would have to travel a distance equal to the radius of Earth—just under 6,400 kilometers (4,000 miles)—before it collided with another air molecule. The exosphere's upper boundary is not clearly defined; this layer gradually blends into the vacuum of interplanetary space within 10,000 kilometers (6,000 miles) of Earth's surface.

Reading Time _2 min_

Recalling Facts

1. Earth's atmosphere is composed of _____ distinct layers.
   - ❏ a. four
   - ❏ b. five
   - ❏ c. six

2. About _____ of the mass of the atmosphere is found within 80 kilometers (50 miles) of Earth's surface.
   - ❏ a. 99 percent
   - ❏ b. 94 percent
   - ❏ c. 89 percent

3. The layer of atmosphere nearest Earth is called the
   - ❏ a. stratosphere.
   - ❏ b. mesosphere.
   - ❏ c. troposphere.

4. The amount of water vapor in the troposphere
   - ❏ a. varies.
   - ❏ b. is about 21 percent.
   - ❏ c. is close to 2 percent.

5. The atmosphere is made up mostly of
   - ❏ a. oxygen.
   - ❏ b. nitrogen.
   - ❏ c. water vapor.

Understanding Ideas

6. From the information in the article, one can infer that the atmosphere is thinnest in its upper layers because
   - ❏ a. there is more short-wavelength radiation there.
   - ❏ b. the temperature is lowest there.
   - ❏ c. the gravitational pull is weakest there.

7. According to the article, interplanetary space is a vacuum. It contains
   - ❏ a. no measurable number of gas molecules
   - ❏ b. only planets.
   - ❏ c. an extremely thin atmosphere.

8. At the top of Mount Everest, mountain climbers feel dizzy because
   - ❏ a. the air pressure and oxygen level are low.
   - ❏ b. they become scared of heights.
   - ❏ c. the short-wavelength radiation is strong.

9. A person would most likely _____ at the top of a high mountain.
   - ❏ a. feel more heat from the sun
   - ❏ b. need a heavy jacket for warmth
   - ❏ c. breathe healthier air

10. One could conclude from this article that
    - ❏ a. the exosphere and outer space are similar.
    - ❏ b. Earth's gravitation exerts the same force on all gas molecules.
    - ❏ c. it is extremely cold in all parts of outer space.

24 B The Ozone Layer

About 10 to 40 kilometers (6 to 25 miles) above Earth's surface, in the stratosphere, there is a unique layer of air. This is the ozone layer, a dense blanket containing a gas that is vital to the health of the planet. The ozone layer protects people and other living things from harmful short-wavelength radiation, especially the sun's ultraviolet rays. Ultraviolet rays can cause skin cancer and other health problems.

Ozone, an unstable gas that is faintly bluish in color, is formed in the stratosphere by the action of solar ultraviolet (UV) light on oxygen gas. The same process that forms ozone molecules (O_3) also allows them to shield Earth from harmful solar radiation. UV light is absorbed when it strikes an ozone molecule, splitting the large molecule (O_3) into smaller ones (O and O_2). Later, these smaller molecules reassemble into ozone.

Since the 1980s, scientists have been observing "holes" in the ozone layer above both polar regions. Ozone is unstable in colder temperatures, and this may be why the layer is most fragile farthest from the equator. This thinning of the ozone layer has alarmed many and become the subject of lively debate. Some scientists speculate that chemicals called chlorofluorocarbons, which are used in cooling systems and aerosol sprays, rise into the atmosphere and destroy precious ozone molecules.

(1 min)

1. **Recognizing Words in Context**

   Find the word *speculate* in the passage. One definition below is closest to the meaning of that word. One definition has the opposite or nearly opposite meaning. The remaining definition has a completely different meaning. Label the definitions C for *closest*, O for *opposite or nearly opposite*, and D for *different*.

   _____ a. examine with scientific devices

   _____ b. make an educated guess

   _____ c. know for sure

2. **Distinguishing Fact from Opinion**

   Two of the statements below present *facts*, which can be proved correct. The other statement is an *opinion*, which expresses someone's thoughts or beliefs. Label the statements F for *fact* and O for *opinion*.

   _____ a. The thinning of the ozone layer is most severe over the polar regions.

   _____ b. Breaks in the ozone layer are a critical problem for humankind.

   _____ c. The ozone layer is located in the stratosphere.

3. **Keeping Events in Order**

   Label the statements below 1, 2, and 3 to show the order in which the events happen.

   _____ a. The ozone layer in the colder air above the poles begins to disintegrate.

   _____ b. A layer of ozone forms in the stratosphere.

   _____ c. Chemical interactions destroy some of the ozone.

4. **Making Correct Inferences**

   Two of the statements below are correct *inferences,* or reasonable guesses. They are based on information in the passage. The other statement is an incorrect, or faulty, inference. Label the statements C for *correct* inference and F for *faulty* inference.

   _____ a. Under normal circumstances, the ozone layer replenishes itself.

   _____ b. All forms of pollution can damage the ozone layer.

   _____ c. Pollution may pose harmful effects we do not yet fully understand.

5. **Understanding Main Ideas**

   One of the statements below expresses the main idea of the passage. One statement is too general, or too broad. The other explains only part of the passage; it is too narrow. Label the statements M for *main idea,* B for *too broad,* and N for *too narrow.*

   _____ a. Holes in the ozone layer could result in higher rates of skin cancer.

   _____ b. Scientists have been studying atmospheric gases for many years.

   _____ c. The ozone layer is a key part of Earth's atmosphere because it blocks harmful radiation.

Correct Answers, Part A ___9___

Correct Answers, Part B _____

Total Correct Answers _____

Flower and Plant Reproduction

Flowers, the harbingers of spring and the glory of gardens, are the reproductive organs of plants known as angiosperms. Angiosperms are among the most advanced plants on Earth. They first appeared more than 100 million years ago, during the time of the dinosaurs.

Flowers are complex structures incorporating both reproductive and sterile tissue. They may be perfect, which in botany means having both male and female organs, or they may be imperfect and contain only one type of organ. The showiest part of the flower, the splash of color often visible from far away, is the corolla, the spiraling cluster of petals whose color, scent, and shape serve to attract potential pollinators—usually insects. The male element, or stamen, is comprised of filaments, each of which supports an anther where the grains of pollen develop. The female elements include the pistil, the seed-bearing organ of the flower.

The flower is the angiosperm's evolutionary solution to reproduction in waterless conditions. No water from any source is necessary to transfer the male gamete, the pollen, to the female gamete, the ovule inside the pistil. A flower begins as a bud, which eventually breaks free of its protective wrapping, the sepals. The corolla, which always has at least three petals, opens wide to the sun and the atmosphere, and the male and female gametes develop and prepare for pollination. During pollination, pollen is moved from the anther on the stamen to a receptive stigma, the opening at the top of the pistil. Once the pollen reaches and fertilizes the ovule, a zygote is formed. The tissues of the zygote begin to differentiate, and the result is a seed, which consists of a plant embryo encased in a protective structure. One fertilized ovule becomes a single seed.

It is often best for flowers to cross-pollinate, or be fertilized by pollen produced by a different bloom. Although this is not a problem in imperfect flowers, in a perfect flower there are several mechanisms that discourage self-pollination. The pollen may mature at a rate different from that of the ovule. The anthers may tip away from the pistil, or the shape of the flower may be suited only to a single pollinator.

Flowers have co-evolved with insects for millions of years. The features that people find so pleasing in flowers—shape, color, and fragrance—often have developed to lure specific types of pollinating insects.

Reading Time _2:10_

Recalling Facts

1. _____ are the reproductive organs of _____.
   - ❑ a. Flowers, angiosperms
   - ❑ b. Angiosperms, flowers
   - ❑ c. Pistils, flowers

2. Which of the following is *not* true of a perfect flower?
   - ❑ a. It includes male and female organs.
   - ❑ b. It includes only female organs.
   - ❑ c. It cannot be self-pollinating.

3. The _____ protect the flower bud as it develops.
   - ❑ a. anthers
   - ❑ b. corollas
   - ❑ c. sepals

4. Which of the following statements is true?
   - ❑ a. As angiosperms have evolved, their flowers have become more beautiful.
   - ❑ b. Many flowers have evolved to attract specific pollinators.
   - ❑ c. Perfect flowers usually self-pollinate.

5. During pollination, pollen is transferred to
   - ❑ a. a stamen.
   - ❑ b. a sepal.
   - ❑ c. a receptive stigma.

Understanding Ideas

6. From the information in the article, you can conclude that pollination takes place
   - ❑ a. before the ovule can be fertilized.
   - ❑ b. before the flower has bloomed.
   - ❑ c. several times in each flower.

7. In flowers the male gametes are grains of pollen, just as in humans the male gametes are
   - ❑ a. red blood cells.
   - ❑ b. sperm.
   - ❑ c. testosterone.

8. You can infer from the article that a decline in the population of a pollinator could result in
   - ❑ a. a decline in the number of flowers that depend on it.
   - ❑ b. a decline in the population of other pollinators.
   - ❑ c. an increase in the number of flowers produced.

9. If pollination does not take place,
   - ❑ a. a flower becomes even more fragrant.
   - ❑ b. the plant soon dies.
   - ❑ c. no seeds are formed.

10. The reproductive tissue of a flower includes the
    - ❑ a. stigma, anthers, and sepals.
    - ❑ b. pistil, anthers, and petals.
    - ❑ c. stigma, pistil, and anthers.

Much of the southwestern United States is a rocky desert of dull mauves, greens, and browns. Its arid environment seems to preclude the possibility of brilliant color. Following the rare cloudbursts that provide most of the annual rainfall in that area, however, springtime draws from the parched sands a spectacular floral array.

Perennial plants native to the desert survive for months at a time in the absence of any measurable precipitation. Shrubs such as brittlebush and desert mallow have extensive networks of roots that absorb every available drop of water from the soil. Plants called succulents, which include cacti, have thick spongy stems that absorb and store water in defense against long dry spells. They offer a magnificent display in the spring—creamy blooms from the saguaro, the prickly pear's showy yellow flowers, and the scarlet blossoms on a barrel cactus. The desert's great glory, however, is its profusion of annual flowers.

Desert annuals germinate from heat- and drought-resistant seeds lying dormant in the soil. Desert marigolds, camphor weed, and desert blazing star are the yellow of sunshine. Lavender and blue Mojave asters, desert lupines, and machaeranthera mirror the sky, and Mexican gold poppies and ocotillo paint touches of fiery orange and red. These and other annuals, such as ghost flowers with their purplish centers, saucer-shaped dune evening primroses, and pink sand verbenas, bring a riot of color to the desert landscape just as late winter becomes early spring.

1. **Recognizing Words in Context**

Find the word *preclude* in the passage. One definition below is closest to the meaning of that word. One definition has the opposite or nearly opposite meaning. The remaining definition has a completely different meaning. Label the definitions C for *closest*, O for *opposite or nearly opposite*, and D for *different*.

_____ a. prevent

_____ b. enable

_____ c. include

2. **Distinguishing Fact from Opinion**

Two of the statements below present *facts*, which can be proved correct. The other statement is an *opinion*, which expresses someone's thoughts or beliefs. Label the statements F for *fact* and O for *opinion*.

_____ a. The muted colors of the desert landscape are dull and lifeless.

_____ b. In the spring, desert wildflowers bloom in a variety of colors.

_____ c. Many kinds of plants can grow in the desert.

3. Keeping Events in Order

Label the statements below 1, 2, and 3 to show the order in which the events happen.

_____ a. Spring storms bring rain to the desert.

_____ b. During the same year, wilting ocotillo drop seeds onto the desert soil.

_____ c. Rainwater activates dormant seeds, and lupines, marigolds, and ocotillo bloom.

4. Making Correct Inferences

Two of the statements below are correct *inferences,* or reasonable guesses. They are based on information in the passage. The other statement is an incorrect, or faulty, inference. Label the statements C for *correct* inference and F for *faulty* inference.

_____ a. Succulents include many kinds of cactus.

_____ b. Desert plants flower when there is adequate precipitation.

_____ c. Desert soil is not fertile enough to grow many kinds of plants.

5. Understanding Main Ideas

One of the statements below expresses the main idea of the passage. One statement is too general, or too broad. The other explains only part of the passage; it is too narrow. Label the statements M for *main idea,* B for *too broad,* and N for *too narrow.*

_____ a. Both perennial and annual flowers bloom profusely in the Southwestern desert in the spring.

_____ b. The seeds of desert annuals lie dormant in the soil until rain allows them to germinate.

_____ c. Some plants can grow in inhospitable environments.

Correct Answers, Part A ___9___

Correct Answers, Part B _____

Total Correct Answers _____

Answer Key

Reading Rate Graph

Comprehension Score Graph

Comprehension Skills Profile Graph

Answer Key

1A	1. b	2. a	3. c	4. b	5. c	6. a	7. b	8. b	9. b	10. b
1B	1. D, C, O	2. O, F, F	3. 3, 1, 2	4. C, F, C	5. B, N, M
2A	1. b	2. c	3. a	4. b	5. c	6. a	7. b	8. c	9. a	10. c
2B	1. D, C, O	2. O, F, F	3. 1, 3, 2	4. C, F, C	5. N, B, M
3A	1. a	2. b	3. c	4. a	5. c	6. b	7. c	8. a	9. b	10. b
3B	1. O, D, C	2. O, F, F	3. 3, 2, 1	4. F, C, C	5. M, N, B
4A	1. b	2. a	3. a	4. c	5. b	6. b	7. c	8. a	9. c	10. b
4B	1. C, O, D	2. F, O, F	3. 2, 3, 1	4. F, C, C	5. B, N, M
5A	1. a	2. c	3. b	4. a	5. c	6. a	7. b	8. a	9. c	10. b
5B	1. O, D, C	2. F, F, O	3. 2, 1, 3	4. C, F, C	5. N, M, B
6A	1. b	2. c	3. a	4. c	5. a	6. b	7. b	8. c	9. a	10. c
6B	1. D, C, O	2. F, O, F	3. S, A, S	4. F, C, C	5. B, M, N
7A	1. c	2. a	3. b	4. c	5. b	6. c	7. a	8. b	9. a	10. c
7B	1. C, O, D	2. F, O, F	3. 3, 1, 2	4. C, C, F	5. B, M, N
8A	1. b	2. b	3. c	4. a	5. a	6. b	7. c	8. a	9. b	10. c
8B	1. O, D, C	2. O, F, F	3. 3, 1, 2	4. C, C, F	5. M, B, N
9A	1. c	2. b	3. a	4. b	5. b	6. c	7. a	8. b	9. c	10. a
9B	1. C, O, D	2. F, F, O	3. 1, 3, 2	4. C, F, C	5. N, M, B
10A	1. a	2. c	3. b	4. b	5. c	6. a	7. b	8. c	9. a	10. b
10B	1. D, C, O	2. F, O, F	3. 2, 1, 3	4. F, C, C	5. B, N, M
11A	1. a	2. b	3. c	4. c	5. a	6. c	7. b	8. c	9. b	10. a
11B	1. D, O, C	2. F, O, F	3. 1, 3, 2	4. C, C, F	5. M, B, N
12A	1. a	2. b	3. a	4. c	5. b	6. c	7. b	8. c	9. c	10. a
12B	1. D, C, O	2. F, O, F	3. 2, 3, 1	4. C, F, C	5. N, M, B
13A	1. c	2. a	3. c	4. b	5. a	6. b	7. b	8. c	9. c	10. a
13B	1. C, D, O	2. O, F, F	3. 3, 2, 1	4. C, F, C	5. B, M, N

14A	1. b	2. a	3. b	4. c	5. c	6. a	7. c	8. b	9. a	10. b
14B	1. O, C, D		2. F, F, O		3. 1, 3, 2		4. C, C, F		5. M, N, B	
15A	1. a	2. c	3. b	4. b	5. c	6. a	7. b	8. c	9. c	10. b
15B	1. C, D, O		2. F, O, F		3. 1, 3, 2		4. C, F, C		5. N, B, M	
16A	1. b	2. c	3. b	4. c	5. a	6. c	7. c	8. a	9. b	10. b
16B	1. O, D, C		2. F, F, O		3. 2, 3, 1		4. C, F, C		5. N, B, M	
17A	1. c	2. a	3. b	4. b	5. a	6. c	7. b	8. c	9. c	10. a
17B	1. O, C, D		2. F, F, O		3. 1, 2, 3		4. C, F, C		5. M, B, N	
18A	1. a	2. b	3. c	4. a	5. b	6. c	7. a	8. b	9. c	10. b
18B	1. C, D, O		2. F, O, F		3. 2, 3, 1		4. F, C, C		5. M, B, N	
19A	1. c	2. b	3. a	4. c	5. a	6. b	7. a	8. c	9. a	10. c
19B	1. D, O, C		2. O, F, F		3. 2, 1, 3		4. C, F, C		5. N, B, M	
20A	1. b	2. c	3. c	4. a	5. c	6. b	7. a	8. b	9. c	10. a
20B	1. O, C, D		2. O, F, F		3. 2, 1, 3		4. C, C, F		5. B, N, M	
21A	1. a	2. c	3. b	4. a	5. c	6. a	7. b	8. c	9. a	10. b
21B	1. C, O, D		2. F, O, F		3. 3, 1, 2		4. F, C, C		5. M, N, B	
22A	1. b	2. b	3. c	4. a	5. c	6. b	7. c	8. b	9. c	10. b
22B	1. D, C, O		2. F, F, O		3. 2, 3, 1		4. C, F, C		5. N, B, M	
23A	1. c	2. a	3. b	4. a	5. b	6. c	7. a	8. b	9. b	10. a
23B	1. O, C, D		2. F, F, O		3. 3, 2, 1		4. F, C, C		5. B, M, N	
24A	1. b	2. a	3. c	4. a	5. b	6. c	7. a	8. a	9. b	10. a
24B	1. D, C, O		2. F, O, F		3. 3, 1, 2		4. C, F, C		5. N, B, M	
25A	1. a	2. b	3. c	4. b	5. c	6. a	7. b	8. a	9. c	10. c
25B	1. C, O, D		2. O, F, F		3. 1, 3, 2		4. C, C, F		5. M, N, B	

READING RATE

Put an X on the line above each lesson number to show your reading time and words-per-minute rate for that lesson.

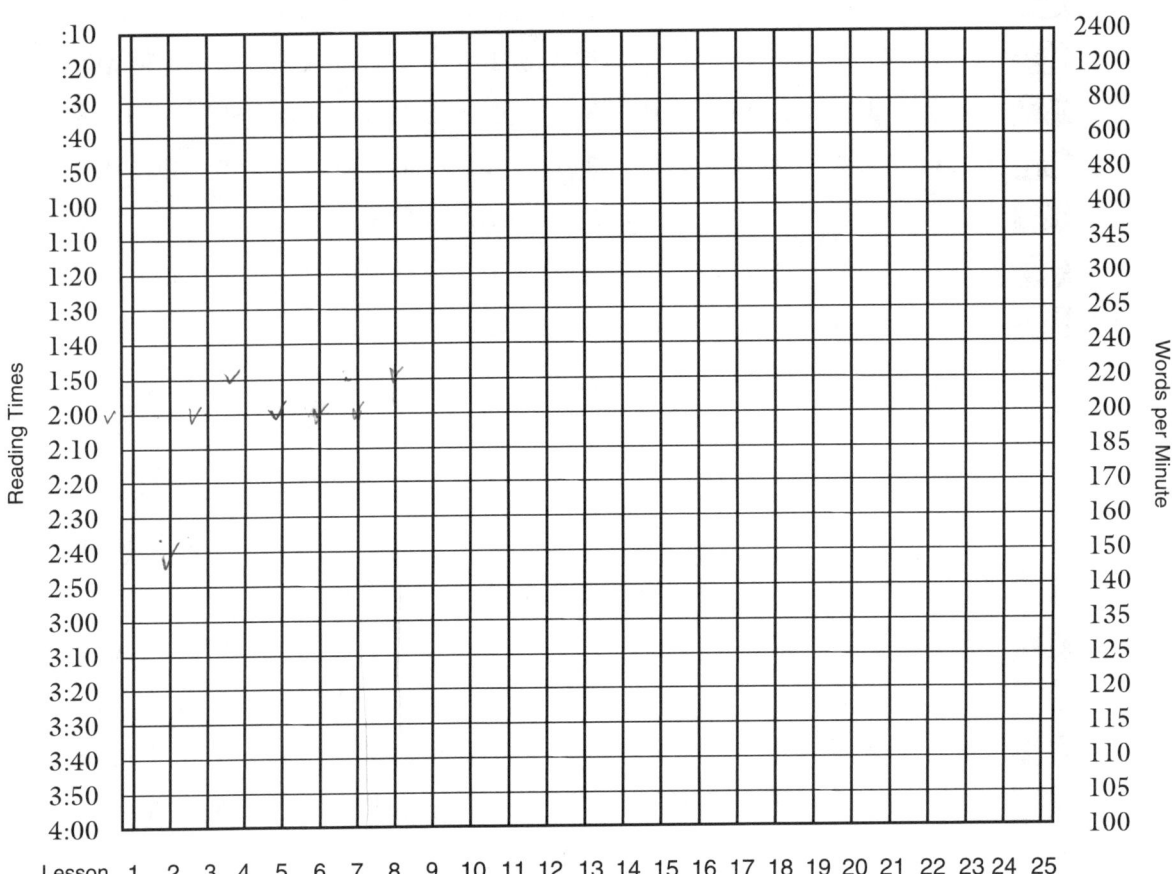

COMPREHENSION SCORE

Put an X on the line above each lesson number to indicate your total correct answers and comprehension score for that lesson.

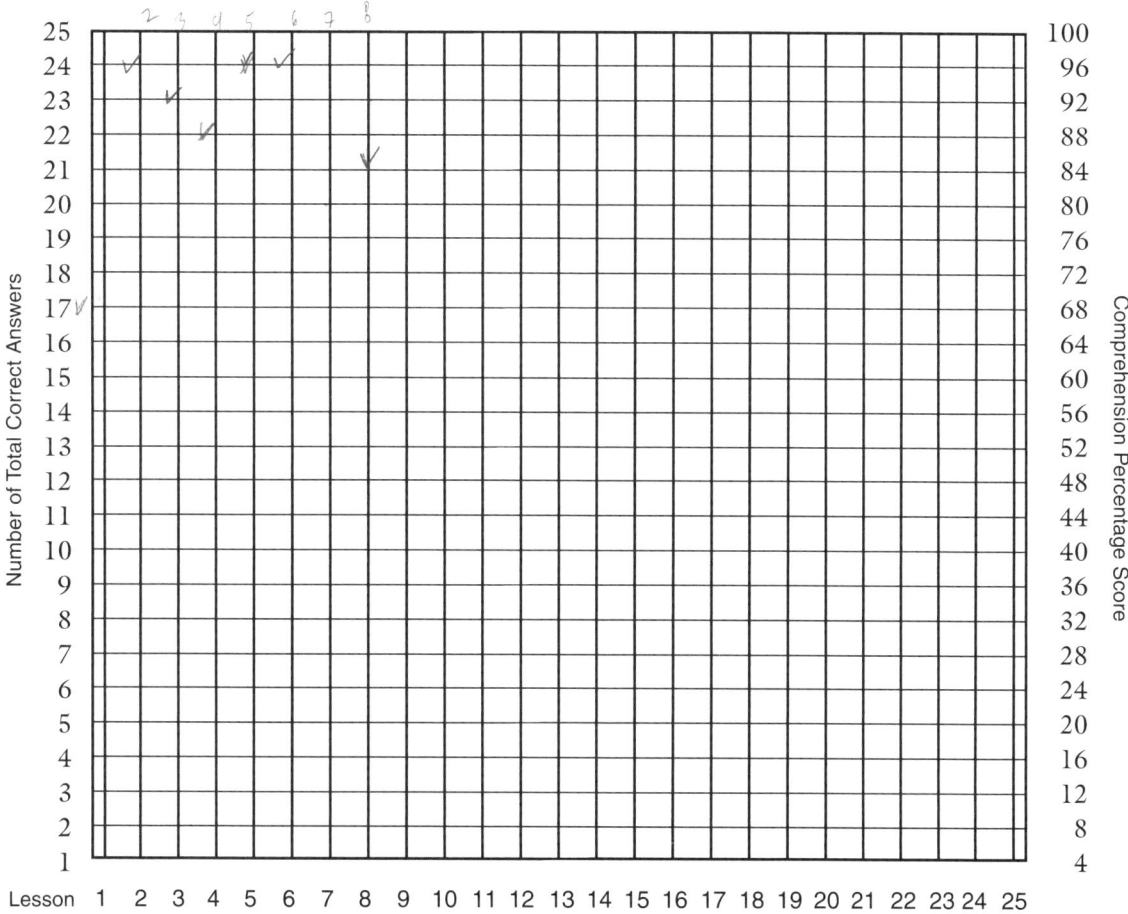

COMPREHENSION SKILLS PROFILE

Put an X in the box above each question type to indicate an incorrect reponse to any part of that question.

Lesson	Recognizing Words in Context	Distinguishing Fact from Opinion	Keeping Events in Order	Making Correct Inferences	Understanding Main Ideas
1					
2					
3					
4					
5					
6					
7					
8					
9					
10					
11					
12					
13					
14					
15					
16					
17					
18					
19					
20					
21					
22					
23					
24					
25					